On Experts: CPR35 for Lawyers and Experts

DAVID S. BOYLE
boyle@deanscourt.co.uk
Deans Court Chambers
24 St. John Street
Manchester
M3 4DF

Law Brief Publishing

Published 2016 by
Law Brief Publishing
30 The Parks
Minehead
Somerset
TA24 8BT

www.lawbriefpublishing.com

Paperback: 978-1-911035-11-4

To Carin and John,

for regularly reminding me
that holding an opinion
does not render one right.

AUTHOR'S NOTE

This book is about opinion. In line with its subject matter, I am well aware that there will be a range of views on nearly every topic that I cover, probably extending to what I've chosen to discuss or exclude. The (normally ignored) requirements of CPR35 are that an expert set out the range of opinion and his position within that range, together with his reasons for adopting that position. I have set out to comply. The opinions that I have expressed represent my true (if not necessarily complete) opinions on the matters to which they refer.

ACKNOWLEDGEMENTS

This book came about because Tim Kevan and Garry Wright at Law Brief Publishing massaged my ego and told me that not only should I write a book but that the first couple of chapters that I produced were good enough to continue the process.

Various people had their brains picked to make sure that specific chapters didn't stray too far off piste: I'm particularly grateful to Paul Currie (ENT reports) and Jon Grundy (Reconstruction reports) who both grunted positively in the early days, whilst making it clear that any errors were, and would still be, mine.

Mary O'Rourke QC gave me guidance regarding FTPPs and Glenn Campbell and others provided sounding boards and cheerleading as necessary as I came up with something new to discuss.

My clerks helpfully appeased some of my solicitors when I was on the final push to finish the draft; Tim Gray, Gordon Exall and Hector Chinoy were good enough to read the preliminary manuscript for review purposes; Mr Justice Turner was generous enough to pen a Foreword; and my very long-suffering friend, David Chart, marked 33 years of friendship and (in his case) intellectual superiority by reading the final manuscript with an expert, but non-legal, eye.

Finally, Carin and John's support (and eye-rolling each time I mention 'the book') has very much served to encourage its eventual completion. My thanks to all concerned. On to the next one!

David Boyle
November 2016

FOREWORD

In June 2016, former Lord Chancellor, Michael Gove declared: "I think people in this country have had enough of experts." Indeed it remains the case that, at the time of writing, experts generally, are having a hard time. Confident electoral and economic predictions appear to be coming to grief again and again.

There is nothing new in this.

According to Shakespeare, 1415 was also a particularly bad year for experts. On the eve of the Battle of Agincourt, Lord Grandpré a "most expert gentleman" measured and studied the English lines. His conclusions led the Constable of France to conclude that if the English really knew what they were doing "they would run away." The English did not, of course, run away but went on to secure a victory which took the lives of 10,000 Frenchmen at a cost of no more than 112 English casualties. One can only speculate on whether the expert Grandpré actually enjoyed a brief chance fully to appreciate the enormity of his miscalculations before he, himself, was slain in the battle the outcome of which he had so confidently and wrongly predicted.

In the forensic context, experts are generally spared such extreme and personal consequences of failure but the impact upon their clients' fortunes (in both senses) can be decisive. So what can go wrong with expert evidence?

Speaking in 1985, Lord Bingham was able to say: "Expert witnesses may be and often are partisan, argumentative and lacking in objectivity but they are not dishonest."

From my own professional experience, swimming, as I have done, in the murkier backwaters of litigation largely uncharted by most Justices of the Supreme Court, dishonesty in expert witnesses is rare but by no means extinct. In one case involving an insurance claim, the validity and quantum of which were both highly controversial, I called an expert accountant to give evidence on behalf of the claimant. On the first day of the trial things were going well. He was giving what appeared to be coherent and convincing evidence. Overnight, however, counsel for the insurers received an anonymous tip off which resulted in the following exchange in cross examination:

Q Were you in the company of the claimant on 12 July this year?

A Yes.

Q In the United States?

A Yes

Q Nevada?

A Yes

Q At the Viva Las Vegas Wedding Parlour where you married her?

A Could I have a glass of water please?

Doubtless, this is an extreme example but experts now, more than ever, have to be particularly vigilant that their reputations can be preserved intact from adverse comments in judgments of the court. In an age in which virtually every High Court judgment is readily available online, no expert enjoys the right to be forgotten. The risk of exposure by virtue of inconsistency is also ever present. An expert who has recently expressed a firm generic view now enshrined in a judgment with a neutral citation number might subsequently find difficulty in explaining in cross examination how his or her opinion has since changed.

Even where, as in the vast majority of cases, experts are presenting honest, unbiased and consistent views, the reports of some are just too long and lacking in substance. I make no apology for using this opportunity as a platform upon which to repeat one of my more curmudgeonly yet heartfelt outbursts from the case of <u>Harman v East Kent Hospitals NHS Foundation Trust</u> [2015] P.I.Q.R. Q4:

"…(i) there is a regrettable tendency for experts to produce reports which are simply far too long. The comments made by Sir James Munby in his article on this topic in [2013] Family Law 816 are as apposite to personal injury litigation as they are to care cases:

"...too many expert reports..., are simply too long, largely because they contain too much history and too much factual narrative... I want to send out a clear message: expert reports can in many cases be much shorter than hitherto, and they should be more focused on analysis and opinion than on history and narrative. In short, expert reports must be succinct, focused and analytical. But they must also of course be evidence based."

In the experience of this Court it is not unusual for care reports, for example, in catastrophic injury cases to exceed 100 pages in length. Very often the same narrative detail can be found repeated in report after report from different disciplines. The consequences are deleterious. All this involves the parties and the Court in spending a disproportionate time reading the reports which results in an increase in costs. Furthermore, the likelihood that important points are lost in the vastness of the context in which they appear is unhelpfully increased;

(ii) against the background of longer and longer reports there is, however, little sign, in some cases at any rate, that the care and attention spent on analysis and opinion, as opposed to history and narrative, is being given commensurate attention and priority; and

(iii) experts should deal with the issues raised by the other side promptly. In this case, the defendant makes a legitimate point in emphasising that neither the claimant's care expert nor educational psychologist dealt with the option of continued residential care in their reports until the joint statements and even then the matter was dealt with in an over concise way. One inevitable consequence of this was that the reasoning of the experts was only finally fleshed out in oral evidence during the hearing. This should not happen."

I would not, however, wish to end my general comments on experts on a sour note. Over three and a half decades, I have had the professional privilege of working with experts in many fields including: hairdressing, bomb making, the polluting effects of sheep dip, the market and fair grants of King John, the effectiveness of suntan lotions, the explosive properties of saw dust, fine art forgery, shotguns, coal mining, dog training and how safe it is to eat lamb chops after their use-by date. I have certainly learnt a lot more from them than they have from me.

But what of this book?

I wonder how many of those who buy textbooks actually ever read the forewords. I know I don't. From my point of view, the foreword would have been the perfect medium for Cassandra to deploy to warn the Trojans about the treachery of the Greeks, confident in the knowledge that no one would ever read it. For those determined few who have got this far, however, it remains for me to commend this work and its author. I have known David Boyle for many years as a former colleague in chambers and he writes as he speaks. He surveys the territory with the advantage of a wealth of experience richly leavened with a generous helping of personal anecdote thereby combining authority with accessibility. I commend it to all practitioners as a real-world guide to the law and practice relating to expert evidence.

Mark Turner
November 2016

Contents

INTRODUCTION

I have, for several years, run the Mini-Pupillage scheme in Chambers. Such schemes are common, allowing undergraduates and graduates alike the opportunity to see what life at the Bar is like, but my hope, in taking it over, was that we might offer a bespoke service which actually taught mini-pupils rather than simply sitting them at the back of a courtroom somewhere, watching what they could have seen had they simply wandered in off the street.

One of the exercises that we set relates to a fatal road traffic accident, based on a real case:

> A is driving a car with B and C sitting in the rear offside and rear nearside seats respectively. None of them is wearing a seatbelt. They are involved in a high speed, head on, collision with another car, driven by D with E as his front seat passenger. Neither of them is wearing a seatbelt. A, C and E are killed, whilst B and D suffer multiple, but non-life threatening, injuries. You are instructed by A's family to pursue a claim against D, who was clearly driving too fast and on the wrong side of the road, but his insurers have taken the point that A was negligent in not wearing a seatbelt. Photographs of the two badly damaged cars are provided.

> In *Froom v Butcher*[1] Lord Denning set out guidance as to the appropriate reduction for contributory negligence in such cases: If wearing a seatbelt would have avoided injury all together, the reduction is 25%. If wearing a seatbelt would not have prevented injury, but would have reduced it, the reduction is 15%. If wearing a seatbelt would have made no difference, there should be no reduction.

> Is the appropriate reduction in the instant case:

---

1   [1976] 1 QB 286

A.	25%?
B.	15%?
C.	0%?
D.	Other (please specify)?
E.	Other (please specify)?

Whilst nobody ever answers A, the vast majority, after some consideration, plump for B or C, depending on the view that they take of the photographs. Few have a stab at D, and even fewer ask themselves the obvious question: "Why am I being offered not one, but two, 'Other (please specify)' options?"

The first answer is, of course, D: "*I don't know.*"

The import is twofold: For the vast majority of students, who have spent hours of study, learning the answers to regurgitate on request in exam conditions, the very idea of professing ignorance is an anathema. Ignorance of the law is no excuse. But this is not a question of law, but a question of fact. It is asked in a legal context, by a lawyer, of a lawyer, but it is a question of fact, and, as lawyers, it is not our job to determine facts – just to consider the evidence before us. That concept has passed the majority of students by, as they spend those long hours in the library, committing case names and references, *ratios* and *dicta*, to memory, all to answer a well-defined, self-contained, essay question in their end of year exams.

In the real world, however, cases are not normally that simple. Back in 2002, in answer to a question at a press conference, the United States Secretary of Defense, Donald Rumsfeld, tried to explain that an absence of evidence is not the same as evidence of a negative. He spoke not only of what the US government knew, but also what it did not, both in terms of what it knew that it did not know and that of which it had no idea. That analysis, often seen as overly complicated, is, in fact, an excellent distillation of human knowledge.

As *per* Rumsfeld's analysis, the first element are those things which we knew that we know: Here, A was not wearing a seatbelt. A died.

Moreover, there are, almost certainly, things that we don't know that we know: What was the physical injury which caused A to die? We probably have that information in the post mortem report. We have the information available to us, but we don't yet know what we know. [2]

When, however, we get to things that we know are beyond our existing knowledge base, things get more difficult: What was the mechanism of that injury? What physical differences would wearing a seatbelt have made? What medical differences would wearing a seatbelt have made? It is at this stage that the wise man accepts what he does not know, and seeks the advice of someone better qualified to form the necessary opinion: an expert.

This book is about Experts. I have deliberately capitalised the word on this one occasion, because they are professional witnesses and are, or should be, men and women of standing in their chosen fields. They should warrant a capital letter when they stray into the forensic process. They should be worthy of respect and they should earn that respect through their expertise, but they are not, for the most part, lawyers, and their role in the forensic process is an unusual one. They have their own rule within the Civil Procedure Rules 1998: CPR Part 35, but that is the formal starting point of what is often a particularly complicated exercise.

This is designed to be a practical, but not a beginner's, guide to expert evidence and I have written it with both lawyers and expert witnesses in mind.

My first hope is that by making lawyers think about why they need evidence from an expert, and how that evidence might fit into the advisory process which they as lawyers undertake, they might become more demanding of their experts.

---

2   There has been much philosophical debate about whether this category is something which we consciously choose not to know, but this is a practical book, and I prefer a variant of Occam's Razor: That the simplest answer should be the starting point. With that in mind, I am referring in this context to facts which are theoretically known and available to us were we to ask the question, but until we ask the question, we do not appreciate that we have the knowledge.

My second aim is to give real guidance to those who might be asked to give expert evidence. What is required of me? Why am I being asked these questions? How should I be approaching this exercise? How can I justify my opinion?

With those two disparate aims in mind, the book is actually in three sections: The first section of this book deals with how parties might obtain expert evidence, the mechanics of doing so and some of the pitfalls which arise.

In the second section, the formalities of expert evidence are considered, together with the practicalities of how to use (and abuse) expert evidence. I hope that both legal practitioners and experts, of whatever standing, might find useful the matters collated and might take something from the sections about how reports should be structured and matters addressed.

The final section of this book is, in many ways, the most difficult and interesting. I have attempted to consider a number of different fields of expertise and proffer my opinions about what a specific type of expert might look to achieve in his report. The list concentrates on experts in the fields commonly seen in personal injury law. I have written about areas which I have dealt with in day to day practice over the last 20 years, and this is a book which deals with experts in civil litigation, giving their evidence in accordance with CPR35. Expert evidence might arise in other forms of litigation: e.g. the expert on DNA evidence in a criminal case or the expert on non-accidental injuries in a family matter, and their duties are potentially different, although I would hope that this book might give them food for thought.

Even so, the list in Part Three is far from exhaustive, and for those whose expertise appears to fall outwith the contents of this book, I ask for understanding and hope that a review of the chapters which do appear will provide sufficient guidance and insight to allow experts to develop their own thought processes on the facts of their specific discipline or the case in question. They are, after all, experts in their own field. If there is sufficient interest, one might see how subsequent editions could be expanded, and I am open to suggestions.

It may be, of course, that there is no correct answer on the facts of any given case. Experts might not agree, each holding firm to his own views. In the real case which gave rise to our problem question, both sides obtained the opinion of an expert in seatbelt issues. They each considered that had A been wearing a seatbelt, he would, on the balance of probability, have survived the initial impact. The problem was that B was unrestrained and that there was a secondary impact from behind. We could not be sure what the nature of that secondary impact was – there had been no contemporaneous analysis and nothing could now be done to remedy that – and it was clearly a very close run thing. Ultimately, the claimant's expert opined that, on balance, A would have died in any event and the defendant's expert opined that, on balance, he would have survived. They held to their views at the joint report stage, and there was nothing to suggest which view was likely to prevail at trial.

In those circumstances, what we actually had was a manifestation of Schrödinger's Cat, the thought experiment where a cat is kept in a locked steel chamber wherein the cat's life or death depends upon the state of a single radioactive atom, which has either decayed and emitted radiation (in which case the cat is dead) or not (in which case the cat is still alive). Until the box is opened, the cat is, in effect, both dead and alive.

In our case, going to court and asking the judge to decide whether A would, on balance, have survived, equates to opening the box, but until that point, both answers are right. As it happened, the lawyers decided that the correct answer was E: 7½%, halfway between B and C. It was not an answer which would have been available to the court, and it was not an answer available to the experts, but it was a practical answer, available to the lawyers, for whom commercial settlement was always on the table. This is, after all, a practical book.

PART ONE

OBTAINING
EXPERT
EVIDENCE

I keep six honest serving-men (they taught me all I knew);
Their names are What and Why and When, and How and Where
and Who.

Rudyard Kipling

CHAPTER ONE
WHY GET AN EXPERT?

Court cases normally involve the interaction of evidence, law and procedure, albeit that often one or more of those aspects withers on the vine. The legal and procedural aspects of the case *should* fall outwith this volume, which concentrates on evidential issues, although there are clearly circumstances where the expert's evidence actually pertains to legal or procedural matters.

In the normal course of events, the parties to litigation are able to provide evidence to the court. Whilst parties are under a duty to disclose relevant documentation,[1] the starting point for evidence is normally a witness statement, setting out the oral evidence which a party would give at trial.[2] That statement must, if practicable, be in the intended witness's own words, should be expressed in the first person, and must indicate which of the statements in it are made from the witness's own knowledge and which are matters of information or belief, together with the source for any matters of information or belief.

Those requirements of 32PD.18 are important, because, if followed properly, they limit a witness's evidence to factual statements. If one writes in the first person, it naturally limits the narrative to matters within one's own knowledge, even if the information is not directly known, but comes from another.[3] Importantly, when one strays into opinion, it is difficult to avoid saying so, either expressly or impliedly.[4] That, in turn, is important because whilst a lay witness can give evidence of fact, he cannot give opinion evidence. It is inadmissible as a matter of law.

---

1   Disclosure is governed by CPR34 and is outwith this book.

2   Lay witness evidence is governed by CPR32.

3   "My neck was sore after the accident. The doctor told me that I had a whiplash injury. I took painkillers and was pain-free the next day. I have not suffered any pain since."

4   "In my opinion, any symptoms that I had in my neck were caused by the accident."

That means that, whenever a litigant needs to prove something beyond his own knowledge, or capacity to give evidence, he needs, in theory at least, evidence from somebody who, as a matter of law, has that knowledge and/or specific skill and competence to opine on the subject. This ties in with the concept of 'judicial notice' whereby if a specific fact is so well known that there can be no doubting it,[5] or is officially recorded,[6] there is no need for formal evidence to be called to prove the point.

In an age where proportionality is fundamental to the litigation process, there is a temptation to presume that the court will take judicial notice of more and more, but there is a very real need to take care not to over-step the mark. It is easily done, but it is not for lawyers, or judges, to impose their personal view of a situation and assume the position of expert in a case. The reason is relatively obvious, but nevertheless often ignored. Whilst we spend our lives making judgment calls on the specific facts before us, if those facts fall outwith our understanding, often because we cannot appreciate the macro scale, we fail to have adequate regard to the bigger picture. Unless one has specific understanding, one cannot comprehend how often an event might take place, and without that comprehension, one cannot simply guess at the effects when it occurs on a specific occasion.

To give an example of our lack of understanding of scale, imagine that the UK appointed an annual Public Philosopher, to whom each person

---

5 E.g. The boiling point of water in normal circumstances. There are, of course, a number of factual issues to be considered, even on this point. What are 'normal circumstances'? It is commonly known that altitude affects the boiling point of water but we immediately see that there are degrees of knowledge. Does it make a difference if one is 500m above sea level? What about 1,000m? How accurate does the answer have to be on the facts of the case? Clearly, if one were looking at whether a specific piece of machinery could operate when the boiling point temperature dropped below 98°C, expert evidence would become critical and an expert would almost certainly be required. If, on the other hand, the question was "Does water from a just-boiled kettle have the capacity to scald?" the Court might take the view that the answer was so obvious that it could take judicial notice. Of course, we now have kettles which heat the water to different temperatures depending on the drink the user wants to make.

6 E.g. The time of the high tide on the day in question.

in the UK paid one penny a week to think radical thoughts on their behalf. 63½M people would pay their weekly penny (because even a child might find a penny) and at the end of the year our philosopher would have been paid £33,020,000. Most people would struggle to understand what that amount of money might actually mean. It isn't lack of intellect or education which restricts that comprehension, but a lack of experience. Time and again we hear of lottery winners who spent everything they'd won – they simply did not understand the meaning of money.

In those circumstances, the question as to whether one needs an expert is, to some extent, a question of judgment for the lawyer, the litigant or the case managing judge. The difficulty is that the judge in question is unlikely to be the tribunal at trial. A district judge, trying to impose a sense of proportionality on a case, might baulk at permitting the parties to spend more than the potential value of the claim on an expert whose evidence might only serve to rubber stamp the contentions made by the litigants, only for the case to take a twist at trial which renders that evidence necessary and the claimant's case (and it will normally be the claimant's case) compromised by its absence.

The court, however, is mandated by CPR35 to restrict expert evidence to that which is reasonably required to resolve the proceedings. There is inevitably an onus on the party wishing to rely on an expert to justify the need for that evidence, and that means that there needs to be a clear understanding of the litigation process and the issues which are going to arise in the specific litigation before instruction is actually made. That normally involves the parties engaging in constructive discussion about what falls to be determined, or, alternatively, the claimant's advisors having a sound basis to believe that the point in issue will need to be resolved in due course.

CHAPTER TWO
WHAT (AND WHO)
IS AN EXPERT?

In simple terms, an expert is somebody who can give opinion evidence. CPR35.2 defines an expert as 'a person who has been instructed to give or prepare expert evidence for the purpose of proceedings' and whilst 'expert evidence' is not defined in the section, it is a given that the evidence will, based on the various factual scenarios which might be relevant, contain opinion drawn from that evidence. It is not, of course, for the expert to usurp the trial judge by reaching definitive findings of fact as to what occurred, or opining as to legal matters (e.g. whether there has been a breach of duty), but the purpose of an expert is to provide the evidential bridge between what we know we know (from the lay evidence) and the conclusions that one cannot draw oneself as a layman.

The status of expert is, to some extent, dependent on the field in question and on what the parties require and are entitled to expect. If the issue is of particular complexity, even a person who has special qualifications and a general interest in that specific issue might not have sufficient expertise. One can see, for instance, that an individual might be suffering from psychological issues, and a psychiatrist (or psychologist) might be instructed to report, but even within the field of psychiatry there are sub-specialisms, such as addictions (e.g. drugs or drink), learning disabilities, psychosomatic conditions and post-traumatic stress disorders. Simply picking somebody who is a qualified psychiatrist is not sufficient.

With orthopaedic medicine the problems can be just as significant. The modern trend is to ever more specialised doctors, whereas those who qualified 20, 30 or even 50 years ago were expected to be generalists who might, in time, develop a specific area of interest. There are cases now where one orthopaedic expert might be instructed to report on the shoulder injury whilst another might report on the knee.[1]

This can cause problems in a case, both for the solicitors and for the experts themselves, not least because many experts are instructed through agencies, particularly when a solicitor finds himself representing a client some distance away. Without local knowledge, or prior experience, of an expert, the solicitor can only ever make enquiries with colleagues (or the legal community as a whole) or ask the experts or the agencies who they recommend. In those circumstances, it is ever more important that the expert is honest, not just on the face of his CV but on receipt of any enquiry or instruction, so that if a case is legitimately beyond his capacity, he simply says so.

One very real problem for those doctors who overstep the bounds of their experience and expertise is that the General Medical Council will potentially call them to account if they proffer opinions outwith their experience. The sanctions can be significant. In *Pool v General Medical Council*[2] the appellant was suspended for a period of 3 months by the Fitness To Practise Panel after he prepared a psychiatric report on a paramedic, A, who was herself the subject of a FTPP. Objection was taken to the appellant's ability to act as an expert in the field and the objection was upheld and the appellant himself charged with misconduct. The point was the appellant was not an expert in the field of general adult psychiatry and had failed to restrict his opinion to areas of which he had expert knowledge of direct evidence. He gave evidence outside his professional competence. He was, in fact, employed as a consultant psychiatrist in the private sector, working in a private hospital. A had been diagnosed as having a personality disorder and post traumatic stress disorder, in part as a result of abuse suffered during childhood. The appellant prepared a report, but A objected on the grounds that he did not have sufficient expertise in the field of personality disorders. That objection was upheld and A referred the appellant to the GMC.

---

1 I have yet to see a specialist in the right, rather than the left, knee. Heaven knows what would happen with toes.

2 [2014] EWHC 3791

On appeal before Mr Justice Lewis, the appellant asserted that one could acquire expertise not simply by formal training and accreditation but by day to day experience, averring that his work in treating people with personality disorder and post traumatic stress disorder sufficed, whether he was working in a secure setting or in the community. Lewis J concluded that the Panel was not wrong in reaching its conclusion. The appellant was not on the Specialist Register in the category of general psychiatry and had not completed any higher professional training. He was not equipped to be an expert. His clinical practice was in the care of offenders and others with similar needs in secure units, and whilst he had considerable experience in the treatment of women with personality disorders, A's case was focussed on the occupational functioning of patients. The Panel's judgment was correct, albeit that the sanction was flawed and disproportionate and the appellant's registration was subjected to a condition that he should not, for 3 months, accept instructions to act as an expert witness in fitness to practise proceedings.

Undoubtedly, that case arose because A felt strongly about the report which sought to go against her in her own disciplinary proceedings. Whether such objection might arise in a personal injury action is a slightly different question. If a claimant has a supportive expert and the defendant's expert does not have equivalent expertise, one would hardly object to his use before he gave his evidence and was cross-examined on the fact that he was outside his normal area. Much, of course, depends on the level of expertise being required of the expert. With respect to those providing reports on soft tissue injuries sustained in minor road traffic accidents, there is a significant upgrading of the level of expertise required if one is asked to opine on the aetiology of a somatoform disorder arising from the effects of two separate accidents being superimposed upon a potentially vulnerable personality. The psychiatrist whose true speciality is, for instance, psychosis, might consider discretion the better part of valour, to be contrasted with the reporting on soft tissue injuries by a radiologist, whose field of expertise, one might argue, is in not seeing the very body parts upon which he is proffering opinion. The fact that the claim for the somatoform disorder might be worth 100 times the minor whiplash is, in all probability, the single most important factor in the level of expertise which one might legitimately expect.

It follows that mere qualification might not constitute expertise, and that specific interest and/or experience is required, but can one be an expert without qualifications? Attendance on even the shortest of courses might now give the attendee a certificate, but does that make one an expert? The answer will depend on the field in question. The onus will be on the person claiming expertise to show that they have within their knowledge and experience, a specific understanding which allows them to proffer a legitimate opinion. In the context of CPR35, as discussed later, the starting point should inevitably be an understanding of the topic which is sufficient to allow the putative expert to set out the range of opinion and then to engage with the facts of the instant case and explain both what his conclusions might be and why he has alighted on his chosen position rather than the others available.

That can lead to specific problems in cases where one side, normally the defendant employer, has employees with particular expertise and training in, for instance, security systems and personal safety. A claimant, arguing a need for equality of arms, might seek expert opinion as to the adequacy of the system in use. Is that 'Expert' an expert in the field? Does that person understand retail? Does that person understand that particular industry? And should that expert have discussions with an employee who is, in reality, giving lay evidence about how and why the defendant's system is in place? There is a very real difficulty in such cases where the employee might, in fact, be more expert than the expert, but cannot be a CPR35 expert because he cannot fulfil his duty to the court. The answer to that lies with the court's approach to the expert, and, importantly, the expert's approach to his reporting. The critical point is, almost inevitably, in deciding where the line falls to be drawn between what is common sense and what is genuine expert opinion, such that no layman could be said to have the requisite knowledge and understanding to form that opinion. The court, and the lawyers, need to be alert to the limitations of the expert, just as he should himself.

CHAPTER THREE
WHEN SHOULD ONE
INSTRUCT AN EXPERT?

This is actually one of the more challenging questions that the lawyer must answer. On the one hand, why would anybody want to engage in litigation without knowing that they were able (at least *prima facie*) to prove the necessary parts of their case? On the other, what is the point of investing significant sums of money in an expert if the issue is not going to be contested or, worse still, the case managing judge will demand a Single Joint Expert or refuse permission to rely on the expert at all?

To give an example, one of the more fashionable areas of personal injury litigation is for Noise Induced Hearing Loss. There are several hurdles for a claimant who wishes to pursue such a claim,[1] but one of the most obvious is that he has, in fact, been exposed to excessive noise (i.e. levels of noise above the level from time to time prescribed), the other being that he has, in fact, suffered some hearing loss consistent with having been exposed to excessive noise. The latter is a matter for consultant ENT surgeons, but the former is the domain of the acoustic engineer.

In a clinical negligence claim, one would inevitably obtain a report on the question of liability before issuing proceedings, because it allows the claimant to know the strength of his case and to formulate the allegations against the defendant. Nobody would dream of doing otherwise. In claims for NIHL, however, courts up and down the land, mindful that they have scores of such matters coming through their doors (and one must bear in mind that the nature of these claims is that they are centred on towns and cities with, historically, heavy industry), have

---

1 Not least in obtaining a constructive response from the potentially numerous defendants and/or insurers who are often inundated with such claims. There are, unfortunately, significant potential benefits to defendants in doing nothing in such claims, not least because, absent sufficient communication in the pre-action phase, the risks to a claimant increase so much that there are many who prefer to walk away from what is potentially a perfectly good claim.

developed standard forms of direction whereby documents are exchanged, witness evidence is exchanged, ENT evidence is obtained (if the defendant wishes to get its own evidence, which it normally does) and exchanged, joint statements from the ENT consultants are provided, and then and only then is the engineer expected to report.

The argument that there needs to be exchange of documents and lay evidence before the report can be obtained is legitimate. One would expect the defendant to provide any documentation in the pre-action protocol phase, although that does not always happen. The other counter-argument sometimes raised by the defendant is that they need more time to locate any witness to give evidence as to how the premises were set up, or how the claimant might have been expected to work. The problem with that argument is that a competent acoustic engineer should be able to opine as to the likely noise levels emanating from certain types of work, and should be able to give a range of opinion as to how certain factual scenarios might affect that. The claimant will, of course, be in a position to provide his own case to the expert, and the expert can prepare his report on that basis. If, in time, the defendant seeks to counter the factual basis of the report, they would be able to ask questions in that regard. Nevertheless, a party should always consider, before instructing an expert, whether there is, as yet, sufficient information upon which he can form an opinion and/or whether that information is likely to become available in time.

To some extent the problem is that, because such cases are now so common place, the current cohort of engineers cannot produce reports quickly enough, and there is an inevitable delay to the litigation whilst the parties await the report. The effect, however, has been to trammel the case managing judiciary to the point where any attempt by the claimant to rely on an acoustic engineer's report already obtained is dismissed as inherently flawed. It is not, because it makes good sense for the claimant not to invest time and money into a case if the engineer's report will come up short, but the courts have taken a view that the more proportionate way to proceed is to frontload the medical evidence and then see whether the noise levels were, in fact, sufficient to found a breach of duty.

In those circumstances, it would appear that the only way in which a claimant can protect himself, particularly pre-action, is to make full use of Notices to Admit Facts and specific Part 36 offers pertaining to individual issues within the case. If a claimant believes that the working environment in any given factory was such that noise levels were dangerously high (perhaps because the solicitors have previous experience of claims against that employer or in respect of similar work), they might reasonably serve a Notice to Admit Facts along the lines of: "You are required, within 21 days, to admit that [this type of work] gave rise to noise levels in excess of 90dB(A)." If the defendant does not admit that fact, there would be potential cost consequences in proving that fact, even if the claim ultimately failed on other grounds. Similarly, one might back up that Notice with a suitable Part 36 offer, say to accept, say, 90% of damages in exchange for the admission of breach of duty, worded in such a way that if the defendant denied the breach of duty, but the claimant proved same, the benefits of Part 36 would attach.

Once protected in such a way, the claimant would have far more confidence in obtaining such engineering evidence because there would be strong arguments that the costs incurred should be paid by the defendant in any event, potentially on the indemnity basis.

Will that protect the claimant who has obtained a report 'prematurely' as far as the court is concerned? There will, of course, be resistance, but one ventures to suggest that faced with a line of correspondence which said: "1. We believe x, do you deny it? 2. We believe x and we would like you to admit it. 3. Please admit x and save us all some bother. 4. You are required to admit x and if you don't, we're going to incur costs to prove it and then get you pay them in any event. 5. Fine, last chance, we'll even compromise a little if you admit this." a case managing judge would have significant sympathy for the claimant who had gone on to incur those costs, and would potentially penalise the defendant by preventing it from obtaining evidence in rebuttal.

Equally, in cases where QOCS (Qualified One-Way Cost Shifting) applies, is it really in a defendant's interest to incur all of the potential costs in a case before deciding whether there is, in fact, a breach of duty? Spending thousands of pounds in costs and disbursements just to see the claimant legitimately fall at the last hurdle, so that the case is lost but without cost penalty, cannot be in the defendant's best interest.

Finally, in deciding when to instruct an expert, one should always have regard to the possibility that if they are instructed too late in the day, they might not be able to report in time, which is almost inevitably going to cause the court concern as to whether to give permission at all.

CHAPTER FOUR
WHERE SHOULD ONE
INSTRUCT AN EXPERT?

This should, of course, be relatively simple. In the majority of cases, there will be sufficient numbers of experts in the field that one should be able to find an expert who is local, either to the claimant (where meeting with the claimant is an integral part of the preparation of the report) or to the accident location (if that is relevant). Much, however, depends on the viewpoint of the instructing party, and the likely cost consequences. A particular firm of solicitors might have a preference for a particular expert, because they perceive that he is more likely to be sympathetic to their point of view. It was ever thus. Many experts now operate clinics throughout the country, allowing them to see clients wherever they may live. The cost of hiring rooms for the day can easily be offset if one is seeing several patients.

In the current climate of proportionality, however, there are potential pitfalls in instructing an expert who will incur substantial travel costs or where, in the case of a badly injured claimant, the logistics of seeing an expert instructed by the defendant might prove difficult. Of course, if the claimant has himself travelled a distance to see his own chosen expert, his resistance to seeing the opposition is somewhat weakened. Ultimately, it will come down to what is reasonable in all the circumstances. If a party can justify instructing an expert 200 miles away and is prepared to pay for the claimant to travel to the examination (or even get the expert to travel to the claimant) then the court is unlikely to interfere unless it is simply too onerous.

There are, of course, cases where a local expert is not appropriate. The most common is a claim for clinical negligence where an expert just up the road might be more likely to know the allegedly negligent treating physician than someone who lives some distance away. That said, it is imperative that one checks with the expert before they accept instructions as to whether the potential defendant is known to them. If, in fact, the defendant trained under the expert 25 years ago, or the expert is good friends with the defendant's wife (who trained under him 25 years ago), geographical distance counts for naught.

Finally, there is the interesting question of where an expert might examine a patient. Traditionally, the patient would attend the doctor's consultation rooms, but for many generic medical reports there is little need for specialist equipment and many simply hire a room in a local conference facility or hotel to allow them the privacy to discuss the case with the client and conduct such examination as is necessary. Whether the report is as cogent when one cannot, for instance, measure height and weight, or observe the claimant walking or moving around outside the confines of the formal examination is another matter. There are, of course, cases where doctors examine the claimant at the claimant's own home. In some circumstances, this is necessary. The claimant may simply be unfit to leave the house, or there may be real merit in the expert seeing the claimant in their natural surroundings, but one must inevitably be wary of such meetings. The expert needs to be objective in their examination and their findings, and the formality of a consultation room can provide that, not least because one can form an expectation of how patients might respond to those particular surroundings. Equally, observing a client in their own home must be an integral part of a care expert's reporting because they need to see what can and cannot be done on a day to day basis.

Ultimately, it is a matter of common sense to decide where the claimant might best be examined. It should go without saying that the offices of the instructing solicitor or the claims management company are inappropriate when one is trying to appear objective.

CHAPTER FIVE
HOW DOES ONE INSTRUCT
AN EXPERT?

Having decided that an expert is reasonably required in the case, and that the time is right to instruct him, how does one actually go about doing it?

The first thing to remember is that instructing an expert is not the same as getting permission to rely on the evidence that one hopes to obtain. The court might well refuse permission, either because the report is unnecessary, or because the expert is not an appropriate person to pass opinion on the issue at stake. For those reasons, and to encourage a cards on the table approach, there are specific Pre-Action Protocols within the Civil Procedure Rules, one of which deals specifically with personal injury claims. That does not mean that all evidence has to be obtained pre-action, as clearly a case can develop over time and new disciplines might be required later in the piece, but it gives an obvious starting point as to how the instructing party (normally the claimant) identifies, or introduces, the expert to be used.

The second question to be addressed is as to whether that report should be obtained on a unilateral basis, or a Single Joint Instruction, pursuant to CPR35.7. There will be reports obtained, pre-proceedings, which are clearly unilateral, and are not, in reality, reports for the purposes of the litigation, but rather advisory reports to decide whether there is actually a case to be had. Of the reports obtained for the purposes of litigation, the most common type of report is that of the unilaterally instructed expert, whether on an agreed basis or otherwise. Alternatively, the court may direct (or the parties might agree) a single jointly instructed expert. Whilst the rules suggest that the source of instructions should make no difference to the opinion proffered, there are a host of reasons why that does not happen in reality, and the Single Joint Expert is considered separately in the next chapter.

THE PROTOCOLS

The Pre-Action Protocol for Personal Injury Claims

The Protocol is, on its own admission, primarily designed for fast track claims, and not just to the personal injury element, although it does not apply to claims which proceed under:

(1) the Pre-Action Protocol for Low Value Personal Injury Claims in Road Traffic Accidents from 31 July 2013;

(2) the Pre-Action Protocol for Low Value Personal Injury (Employers' Liability and Public Liability) Claims;

(3) the Pre-Action Protocol for the Resolution of Clinical Disputes; or

(4) the Pre-Action Protocol for Disease and Illness Claims.[1]

If the claimant values the claim beyond the upper end of the fast track, the claimant should notify the defendant as soon as possible, but the spirit of the Protocol should still be followed.[2] The parties are expected to follow the Protocol and the court may impose sanctions if the parties fail to comply.

In the context of the instruction of experts, the relevant section starts at paragraph 7.2 which makes it clear that, save for cases likely to be allocated to the multi track, the Protocol encourages joint selection of, and access to, quantum experts and, on occasion, liability experts, but makes it clear that the expert report produced is not a joint report for the purposes of CPR35 — that is a different issue. The idea is that the claimant obtains a report and discloses it to the defendant, and they then agree it or ask questions of the expert.

Before instructing an expert, a party *should* give the other party a list of the name(s) of one or more experts in the relevant speciality whom they consider to be suitable to instruct[3] although medical reports are often obtained through agencies. The defendant's consent should be sought

---

1 Pre-Action Protocol for Personal Injury Claims (PAPPIC), paragraph 1.1.1

2 *Ibid* 1.1.2

3 *Ibid* 7.3

and, if requested, the agency should provide the names of the doctors being considered.[4]

Within 14 days[5] of provision of the list, the other party may indicate an objection to one or more of the experts and the first party should then instruct a mutually acceptable expert. If the defendant objects to all of the listed experts (and there may only be one) the parties may then instruct experts of their own choice, with the court deciding subsequently (if proceedings are issued) whether either party has acted unreasonably.[6] If, for instance, the claimant proposes only one expert on the question of liability, and the defendant identifies why it objects to that expert, the court may well disallow that evidence if the claimant goes ahead and obtains a report, even if that means that the claimant's money has been wasted. The objection need not spell out in detail why it objects, but clearly the position is strengthened by a cogent explanation.

If the defendant does not object to a nominated expert they shall not be entitled to rely on their own expert evidence in that field unless the claimant agrees, the court directs, or the claimant's expert's report has been amended and the claimant refuses to disclose the original.[7] This last point is well worth considering. Sometimes it is obvious from a reference number that the report is not a first copy, but there is no reason why the question of amendment should not be asked in any case.

Questions can be asked within 28 days, for the purpose of clarification of the report (see Chapter 11) and answers should be sent simultaneously to each party. The cost of the report is usually paid by the instructing first party, the cost of answering questions by the questioning party.[8] Ultimately, further expert reports can be obtained, albeit that it is a matter for the Court to decide whether the costs of more

---

4   *Ibid* 7.4

5   35 days if the nominations are contained in the Letter of Claim

6   *Ibid* 7.7

7   *Ibid* 7.8

8   *Ibid* 7.10

than one expert's report should be recoverable. It is for that reason that the claimant's solicitors often utilise the first expert instructed (often a general practitioner) to identify the specialities which might subsequently be required.

The Pre-Action Protocol for Low Value Personal Injury Claims in Road Traffic Accidents from 31 July 2013

Where an accident occurred on or after 31 July 2013, this Protocol applies to any claim under £25,000 excluding vehicle related damages. The passage of time and the provisions of section 11 of the Limitation Act 1980, now make this Protocol ubiquitous.

This Protocol is designed to control the use and cost of medical reports, ensuring that in most soft tissue cases only one report is obtained at a fixed cost[9] although additional medical reports may be obtained where required.[10]

Under paragraph 7.3, the claimant must check the factual accuracy of any medical report before it is sent to the defendant. There are a whole host of issues with this provision (and indeed, the entire Protocol system, which is designed to streamline (and thus reduce the cost of) the process for bringing claims, but tends to fail claimants whose cases fall out of that procedure). If the solicitors are being paid a fixed (and modest) fee, and it is unlikely that the doctor (who is also being paid a fixed (and modest) fee (subject to his arrangement with any medical agency)) is going to want to engage in carefully considered amendments of apparently trivial issues within the factual section of the report, what chance is there that a claimant's protestations of minor factual inaccuracy on the face of the report (assuming that they can read it and have read it) will result in an amendment, particularly given that the pre-amended report might be disclosable in any event? What might not be considered an insurmountable problem at that early stage can become an embarrassment for the claimant who finds himself being cross-examined about the report because his credibility is in issue. Rarely does a trial Judge have sympathy with the suggestion that the claimant has

---

9 Pre-Action Protocol for Low Value Personal Injury Claims in Road Traffic Accidents from 31 July 2013 (PAPRTA), paragraph 3.2

10 *Ibid* 7.2

not read the report and even less often are the failings of the experts reporting appreciated or criticised.

Paragraph 7.4 requires the expert to set out the medical records which have been reviewed and the records considered relevant to the claim, all relevant records being disclosed to the defendant with the report[11] but paragraph 7.5 makes it clear that in most claims under £10,000, it is expected that the expert will not need to see any medical records. That, again, leads to a problem, because if a doctor fails to ask the correct question of the claimant about, for instance, whether he has had any previous accidents, injuries, symptoms or claims, and records something less than the truth, then as and when the defendant obtains the claimant's records (often because they have undertaken data searches which suggest that the claimant has, in fact, had a number of accidents), the report is hopelessly compromised. The answer, of course, is for the solicitor to ask the question of the claimant before they are sent to the doctor and ensure that the doctor is made aware of the pre-accident (and post-accident) history, but whether that is cost-efficient is another question.

In non-soft tissue injury claims, any subsequent report from the reporting expert must be justified, either because further time is required before a prognosis can be determined, the claimant is having ongoing treatment or the claimant has not recovered as expected in the original prognosis.[12] Whether that might cause the reporting expert to give an extended initial prognosis is a matter for debate.

In soft tissue injury claims, the expectation is that only one medical report will be required, which will only be justified where it is recommended in the first expert's report and that report has been disclosed to the defendant and both the first and subsequent report was a fixed cost medical report from an orthopaedic surgeon, an A&E consultant, a general practitioner or a physiotherapist.[13]

---

11 *Ibid* 7.4

12 *Ibid* 7.8

13 *Ibid* 7.8B

The Pre-Action Protocol for Low Value Personal Injury Claims (Employers' Liability and Public Liability) Claims
Similar provisions apply to personal injury claims under £25,000 arising from accidents at work or public liability claims, but without provisions equivalent to paragraph 7.5 of the RTA Protocol (the expectation that medical records will not be sought in cases under £10,000).

THE INSTRUCTION

The party instructing an expert needs to have in mind that the letter of instruction may well be read by the other side, or the judge. There is some argument the letter of retainer should be a different document, so as to maintain, if possible, privilege in the latter, although one would hope to be able to deal with such matters transparently.

The letter of instruction itself often takes a standard form, hardly surprising given the nature of bulk personal injury practice, and lawyers will normally use template letters, but whether the evidence being sought is a standard form report or consideration of a unique set of circumstances, the basics remain the same.

The letter should start by identifying the instructing party, both the lay client and the lawyers, and should provide a brief background to the case. Importantly, it should identify what it is that the expert is being asked to report about, and if there are specific points which might arise, they should be identified clearly. Documents should, of course, be supplied to the expert if they are available, or reference made to documents which might be available, but are not currently to hand. Any relevant deadline should be set out clearly and any conditions which might apply to the instructions (e.g. to whom the report will be disclosed) should be identified. Finally, the basis of payment should be made clear.

All of those points should be fairly straight-forward, but it is worth considering why each point might be relevant and setting out some of the more common pitfalls.

As to the identity of the lay client, this should not be too difficult, but there are cases where changes of name cause complications, particularly when one is considering a set of medical notes which appear to relate to somebody else. The identity of the solicitors should be obvious on the face of the letterhead, but there are occasions where instructions are provided through an agency and the solicitors might be unaware of what has been sent through to the expert. Making sure that the report and the instructions marry up, particularly in terms of the factual background and the documents provided, is the key here.

One of the single biggest flaws in using a standard letter of instruction arises when there is a non-standard element to the factual background to the case, but the person sending the letter either doesn't appreciate that, or is ignorant of the import. Even in straight-forward whiplash cases, there might be issues about previous accidents or symptoms, subsequent accidents, the extent of the damage and/or the nature of the impact. It should be the work of an instant for a solicitor to ask the client whether there are any other accidents which the expert might need to consider and yet it is rarely done, apparently in the name of cost (and not even cost-efficiency). It is not difficult to see why that might be important. If the claimant goes to see an expert in June about his accident in March and presents with a stiff and sore neck, but forgets to mention that he had another bump in May, he risks losing his entire claim. If the expert has a letter which says: "*For the avoidance of doubt, the claimant has been involved in **two** accidents this year, one in March and another in May. We are only instructed in respect of the former.*" there can be no doubt that the expert should be able to deal with the report and provide a competent opinion. If he does not, the fee earner should be able to identify that there is a potential problem before the report is sent off to the client.

The second problem arises in cases where the instructing party has not, in fact, turned his thoughts to the reasons why the expert is being instructed in the first place. In more complicated cases, the expert might be instructed at a point in time when the Court has already given directions and identified the issues which fall to be considered by the expert. The chances are that if an expert reports at length on something which is either trite, or not immediately relevant, he will struggle to get his fees.[14] One of the under-appreciated arts of litigation is the distillation of salient issues, honing the questions to be answered to present a party's case in its best possible light. Even a two minute pause for thought as a fee earner can have a massive effect on whether the letter to the expert does the job properly, or is merely adequate. The problem with the latter is that if one reads a report and then tries to decide whether the correct question has been asked, the answer is tainted by the report, and it is harder to identify the question in its purest form.

The third, and often the most important, issue is the documentation sent to the expert. Clearly, the expert needs to have before him clear, cogent, written evidence as to what the case is about. The importance of the evidence being in writing is that there is no doubt about what is being said, and the importance of that evidence being set out on the face of the instructions, and the face of the report, is that all sides know exactly what has been seen by the expert and what might have influenced his decision. It is equally important to realise that anybody reading that report will look at the list of documents to which the expert has been referred and will want to see them. If they are *prima facie* privileged (e.g. a draft witness statement or the report of a previous expert who has not been disclosed because he is not being relied upon) then privilege is waived by the inclusion on the face of the report and the document will have been provided to the other side. There is no point in going to the trouble of a second instruction to get around the opinion of the first expert to be instructed if one simply sends that report to the expert and he makes reference to it. One can be slightly

---

14 The answer, from the expert's point of view, if he feels that he has been asked the wrong question, is to seek guidance from the court using CPR35.14. Reading the rule, there is no requirement for a formal application by the expert, who, it is said, "may file written requests for directions for the purpose of assisting them in carrying out their functions", although they must also (unless the court order otherwise) provide copies before filing them with the court (7 days for the instructing party, 4 days for other parties), and clearly this is designed to give the lawyers the opportunity to provide the expert with the necessary guidance without troubling the court. One suspects that this is one of those situations which one only recognises when it arises, and the questions are likely to be fairly obvious. A simple letter should suffice, addressed to the judge making the original case management order giving permission for the expert.

more sanguine about draft (lay) witness statements being used, because if they are changed because there is a factual error in there, the expert can be asked whether that specific point makes a difference. The court will have to decide whether the draft statement was accurate or not, and will listen to the evidence in that regard, but it is not fatal to the case. Indeed, having lay evidence disclosed as a document in the first instance, rather than as a witness statement, suggests a degree of faith in its validity. There are potentially added advantages to be had, particularly if, for whatever reason, the witness is not going to be cross-examined at trial but the documentation is before the court.

Before leaving the question of documents to be provided, it is, of course, worth noting the position as to the medical records. There is a colossal tension between the premise that the expert need not and will not see the medical records in a soft tissue claim arising from a road traffic accident and the need for an expert to prepare a report on the best evidence that is available to him. As discussed in Part Two, if the medical records are one of only 3 sources of information and are, potentially, more objective than the claimant's history or even presentation on examination, how can it be sensible or reasonable to opine in their absence? Equally, why should a claimant's solicitor spend money on obtaining medical records if they are not going to get paid for them?

One answer might be to make it clear to the insurer, before instruction of the expert, that the expert is not going to be provided with the medical records unless the insurer confirms that it wants those records considered and will pay the cost of obtaining those notes and review thereof. That solves the problem, and is the way that such cases tend to progress in cases where, for instance, low velocity arguments are raised by the insurers upon receipt of the claim. The difficulty is that insurers are unlikely to want to go beyond the basic costs payable, and those costs are so modest that claimants' solicitors are unlikely to want to spend time discussing the matter. The same problem attaches to the experts themselves.

The alternative might be for the solicitors, with their initial correspondence with the client, to include a suitable questionnaire which asks specifically about previous accidents and attendances on medical professionals, before the doctor is instructed. The benefit would be that if the client made reference to GP visits, or previous accidents, simple investigations could be instigated. A letter to the GP asking for the relevant page of GP notes and, perhaps, the last 3 years of entries is neither difficult, nor unreasonable.

The main problem might well be the clients themselves, particularly in low value road traffic claims where there is, in many quarters, a feeling that a claim for compensation should be quick, simple, and without resistance.

Finally, on this point, it is worth noting that CPR35 only applies to those reports which are prepared 'for the purposes of litigation'. In theory, one can always ask an expert to produce a report for advisory purposes, rather than for litigation. The risk is that if one does not use that 'advisory' report, the costs are thrown away because it is not a report obtained in furtherance of the claim.

That said, in cases where the likely conclusion of the report is not relatively obvious when the expert is instructed, asking the expert to produce a 'draft report' (i.e. not one for the purposes of litigation) will allow consideration of those preliminary findings and discussions before the report is finalised. It is a nuanced situation, because the court might disallow that report, and the party might lose the chance to use an expert sympathetic to his case. There is also a potential cost involved in obtaining such a report, reviewing it and then rewriting it, which might mean that the full cost is not recovered from the other side.

That means that this step is unlikely to happen in cases where the injury is a relatively straight-forward whiplash claim, but in cases where the report is critical to the claimant's case on, say, causation, the best practice would be to ask the expert to produce a draft report (which is privileged) and then work with that document, discussing it and ultimately ensuring that it is amended to reflect its status as 'for the purposes of litigation' before disclosing it. Further discussion on that point is to be found in Chapter 11.

What to do with the Report

The Protocols all refer to clients being asked to read and confirm the reports as being true. Appreciating that the cases which get to court represent only the very tip of the iceberg, the number of mistakes which are made in basic GP reports is astonishing. Factual errors such as the position within the car simply should not occur, and it is often unclear as to whether the fault lies with the client or the doctor. The impression is often that the doctor has seen multiple clients from the same accident, but that does not mean that he should simply cut and paste the history given by the first into the other reports. The alternative is that the client simply hasn't read the report, either because they see the report as nothing more than part of a process which is supposed to be hassle-free, or because, as often happens, they struggle with reading, but do not want to admit it.

The problem comes because by the time that witness statements are taken and the claimant is asked about the specific factual inaccuracy, it is too late – the report has been disclosed and the damage is done.

How does the lawyer avoid those errors in the first instance? The obvious way is to ask the questions of the client before the examination. Doctors often use questionnaires to get the client to give their version of events before the examination, to facilitate efficiency. If the initial questionnaire taken by the solicitors has a diagram of a car, and the client is asked to give the name of the person in each seat, it is the work of a moment, but there is then a permanent record, privileged in the first instance, setting out the client's case. If the client says that he's in the rear nearside seat (and has indicated that on the drawing) and the report says that he's in the front passenger seat, it should not be difficult to identify that inconsistency and make sure that the report is accurate before it is disclosed.

It is, of course, worth bearing in mind that if there are inaccuracies in the report, or it has to be changed, there is the potential for the defendant to ask to see the original version of the report. Having a pre-report questionnaire would make it clear that the original report contained an error.

It is often suggested that the problem is that the doctors who produce large numbers of reports baulk at being asked to amend their reports. The answer is a simple one – get them right first time and you won't have to.

CHAPTER SIX
SINGLE JOINT EXPERTS

CPR35.7 allows the court to direct that if two or more parties wish to submit expert evidence on a particular issue, that evidence should be given by a single joint expert. The court can decide who that expert should be, or how the identity of that expert should be decided, if the parties cannot agree on who should prepare that report.

The Practice Direction to CPR35 sets out the factors to which the court should have regard in making decisions about expert evidence and whether to order a single joint expert.

The first issue to which the court will have regard is whether it is proportionate for each party to have separate experts on that specific issue, having regard to the amount in dispute, the importance to the parties and the complexity of the issue. That is simply a reflection of the Overriding Objective, but it is worth noting that it pertains to the particular issue to be considered by that expert. Whilst it might be proportionate for both sides to have their own expert on, say, the prognosis for a damaged joint, is it really going to be necessary to have two separate experts opining on the prognosis for the scarring which results from the surgery?

Moreover, the wording 'separate experts for each party' allows the court to consider whether, in a given case, some parties might jointly instruct an expert whilst others should be outside that instruction. The classic case is where a claimant claims damages for a disease (e.g. Noise Induced Hearing Loss) where there are multiple defendants. There might be an argument as to noise levels, or the apportionment between the defendants, where a single, jointly instructed, engineer might be imposed upon all the parties, but the court might also order that the various defendants jointly instruct an ENT surgeon to counter the claimant's medical expert.

The second issue is whether the use of a single joint expert will assist the parties and the court to resolve the issue more speedily and in a more

cost-effective way than separately instructed experts. This is a potentially difficult area, because there will be cases (e.g. head injury cases)
where repeated neuro-psychological testing within a short space of time
will skew the results on the second examination, rendering it unreliable.
To give parity of arms to the defendant (as it is normally the claimant
whose expert examines first) causes an inevitable delay. The potentially
unattractive alternative, however, is to impose a single joint expert in a
case where the brain injury might be of significant value and the
claimant's solicitors, understandably, want to have control over the
evidence in that regard. Moreover, where the expert is likely to be central to the determination of the case, a party would understandably want
to be able to confer with the expert and test that evidence before going
to court. The court has the power to impose a single joint expert, but
much will depend on the views of the parties. If both parties are resol-
utely against the idea and can give good reasons for that, the court
should be slow to interfere, but a different judge on a different day
might take a different view. Other factors are likely to become relevant
in such circumstances.

The third issue to which the court should have regard given 35PD.7 is
whether the evidence is being given on the issue of liability, causation or
quantum. In each case, the court will have to have one eye on whether
the issue is likely to be dispositive, and the court will be careful not to
box itself in — it is not the expert's job to decide a case. If the court is
of the view that a single joint expert is appropriate on that issue, the
parties will need to encourage the court to define the extent of the
expert's report with care, advising the court of all relevant issues (and
the expert's take on them) but ensuring that the court still has free rein
over the decision-making process.

There are numerous scenarios where the court might consider that a
single joint expert on liability is appropriate. One seen on a regular basis
is the case where an employee, who suffers injury at work when his
workplace is targeted by a robber, seeks to introduce evidence as to the
reasonableness of the security measures in place. The court might feel
that some sort of expert evidence is appropriate in those circumstances,
as to industry standards, the potential cost and the potential benefits

and difficulties which any given step might have. The difficulty comes in knowing where to draw the line. Is the expert the right person to comment on the methodology of a risk assessment? What data should be considered? Is a change in industry standard actually for the better, or just a trend? The defendant might have its own view on such points and may have its own lay evidence which the court will have to consider, and the difficulty is as to whether the expertise of the lay witness renders his opinion evidence admissible. He may, of course, have more expertise on the specific point than the expert.

It is imperative in those circumstances that the issues on which the expert is instructed to opine are closely defined. Moreover, even if the expert is a single joint expert, that does not mean that he is immune from cross-examination or the rejection of his evidence. He must be careful not to place himself in the position of advocate for one side or the other. The problem arises because the judge making the case management order for expert evidence may never have seen such a case before. The onus in those cases is surely on the parties to explain at the CCMC the precise issues upon which the evidence is sought and the reasons why a single joint expert is, or is not, appropriate.

A scenario where evidence is normally given by a single joint expert is engineering evidence in Noise Induced Hearing Loss claims. There, the question is whether, from the lay evidence, the noise levels were likely to be injurious, and, following on from that, whether the exposure (and therefore the injury) can be proportioned between different defendants. Those reports go to both liability and factual causation, but not medical causation, which is another matter.

In cases where the evidence in question goes to medical causation, single joint experts are relatively rare, because medical causation is often the single most determinative issue in the case, so the parties tend to want to maintain control over the evidence. The court may take a different view, but should have in mind the questions: "What is the point of getting this evidence? What might be the range of opinion? How sure can one be that the expert in question is going to assist in that regard?" Those questions should arise in every case, but are often left unasked or, worse, unanswered. One case where such a course is potentially useful is where there is one preeminent expert in the field, and the parties would both want to utilise his services. There are occasional medical conditions which are so specialised that there are acknowledged experts, to whom other more generalist experts defer. Both sides might, for instance, have an orthopaedic surgeon who can opine on the claimant's general condition, but a single jointly instructed expert might be the best person to opine as to the benefit of specific surgery.

In cases where the question goes to quantum, there is often real scope for the use of a Single Joint Expert, particularly when the issue is a relatively straight-forward one of valuation. Again, the court should make it clear as to what is required of the expert when giving that permission.

This ties in with the fourth issue to which the court must have regard under the Practice Direction – the extent to which the expert evidence falls within a substantially established area of knowledge which is unlikely to be in dispute or whether there is likely to be a range of opinion.

The fifth issue is whether a party has already instructed an expert on the issue in question and whether or not that was in compliance with a practice direction or protocol. If a party has taken pre-action advice on the viability of the claim (which advice might be privileged, which is the eighth point raised) and then seeks to utilise the services of that expert within the claim, only for the other side to disagree with his evidence, either on principle or by reference to its contents, the court may be uncomfortable at letting the party rely on that evidence as if it were, and had been obtained as, expert evidence. The court might, in those circumstances, allow the party the benefit of expert evidence on that topic, but not from the expert previously instructed, and impose a single joint expert on the parties, again with a specific remit.

The sixth issue to be considered is whether CPR35 questions might alleviate the need for a second expert, whilst the possibility of the single joint expert giving evidence at trial is the seventh.

The danger, in all such cases, is that a party which is dissatisfied with the opinion of the single joint expert will instruct a shadow expert. Such concerns were highlighted at the time of the Woolf reforms, because lawyers were unsure as to how a single joint expert could maintain neutrality, but have been relatively rare in practice. The questions of cost, and cost-efficiency, mean that only in the rarest of cases will parties go to the expense of getting their own expert to undermine a single joint expert, but in those cases the evidence of the single joint expert often starts to unravel as a result of carefully phrased Part 35 questions, or the party who is dissatisfied with his evidence will apply to the court to rely upon their own new evidence.

THE INSTRUCTION

CPR35.8 sets out the way in which a single joint expert should be instructed. Any relevant party may give instructions to the expert[1], but must, at the same time, send a copy of those instructions to all other relevant parties.[2] The court may give directions about the payment of the expert's fees and expenses[3] (in the first instance, as they potentially follow the event in the long run), and any inspection, examination or experiments which the expert wishes to carry out.[4] The court can limit the fees to be paid to the expert[5] and may even direct that some or all of the relevant parties pay that amount into court,[6] but the default provision is that the relevant parties are jointly and severally liable for the payment of the expert's fees and expenses.[7]

The purpose of CPR35.8 is to ensure transparency in the parties' dealings with the expert. It is that very transparency which makes parties,

1   CPR35.8(1)

2   CPR35.8(2)

3   CPR35.8(3)(a)

4   CPR35.8(3)(b)

5   CPR35.8(4)(a)

6   CPR35.8(4)(b)

7   CPR35.8(5)

particularly claimants, cagey about the use of single joint experts in the first place.

It follows that when a single joint expert is to be instructed, particular care needs to be exercised in the content of the instructions, and if a party feels that particular issues need to be considered, they should set them out openly on the face of the letter of instruction and include any relevant documentation for the benefit of the expert. If the point is a good one, there should be no need to lead the expert to that conclusion – the matter should speak for itself, and, once raised, the expert will struggle to ignore it. If the expert does not accept the contention, then the party may need to ask CPR35 questions, or even cross-examine the expert as to why he has rejected what is, in the party's eyes, a good argument, but an attempt to force a single joint expert to reach a pre-defined conclusion is a dangerous game to try to play.

CHAPTER SEVEN
ON RECEIPT OF INSTRUCTIONS:
THE EXPERT

The way in which an expert should approach the writing of a report is dealt with in detail in Chapters 9 and 10, but at this point it is worth considering the response from an expert when he is instructed and what, if anything, should be done differently by an expert who is jointly instructed?

Unilateral Instruction

The first point is that there should be a clarity of instruction. The letter should make it clear whether the report is for advice purposes only, or whether it is to be a CPR35 report for the purposes of proceedings. If the latter, the letter of instruction should comply with the various aspects of the Protocol (see above, Chapter 5), and the expert should ensure that it does. If the expert has questions, he should ask at an early stage. If there is a glaring omission from the instructions, or there are documents which are missing from the instructions, that should be raised as soon as possible upon receipt. If there are other documents which are potentially important, they should be sought sooner rather than later. Indeed, if one party has access to information which is not reasonably available to another party, the court may direct that the party with access to that information file and serve a document recording that information.[1]

The second point is that the deadline for the report should be noted and explanation proffered if the expert cannot make that deadline. In pre-proceedings instructions, this is rarely an issue, but if Limitation is an issue, there is nothing worse from the solicitor's point of view than waiting for the expert to report when there is an immovable deadline for service of documents.

---

1 CPR35.9. This should not, however, be used by the expert to go off on a frolic of his own to try to prove his pet thesis. The risk is that not only will he not be paid for his efforts, but that a disgruntled party, perceiving him to have lost objectivity, will apply for him to be removed as an expert. The question is, as ever, one of proportionality having regard to the issues in the case.

Thirdly, the expert should consider whether he is, in fact, an appropriate expert to advise in the case. There is always a fear that saying 'No' will restrict further instructions, but the reality is that if a solicitor understands that he can trust the expert to say when he is and when he is not able to opine, he will get more instructions, because his understanding of the issue will potentially set him apart. It may be that he knows somebody who does have a specific interest in the area in question. One would not want to realise, halfway through a case, that the other side had instructed that particular expert, who knows far more about the topic, only for instructing solicitors to ask the question: "Why didn't you tell us to go to Dr X when we first came to you?"

Fourthly, the expert should consider the instructions, and in particular the specific points on which he is asked to advise. If he feels that the question is phrased incorrectly, or that he is straying beyond his expertise, he should say so as soon as practicable. If there is a nuanced difference between the question which he has been asked and the question which he feels is the real question in the case, it may be down to a subtle lack of understanding on the part of the instructing party, but the parties may not take issue with that point. If so, it is better that the expert understands that as early as possible so that he might report efficiently.

The fifth point to bear in mind is that there might be a conflict of evidence in the case which might change the expert's approach to the question. On a unilateral instruction, that may not be obvious, and the expert should not set about his own investigations in that regard. He should simply ensure that he has taken a proper history from the claimant so that he is reporting on the appropriate set of facts. The more interesting issue arises in the case of a single joint instruction as set out below.

Finally, it is a fairly trite point that the basis of the retainer should be agreed at this point. Is the expert to charge a flat fee for the report? Is he to charge an hourly rate? Has the court placed a limit on the cost of his report? If so, can he fulfil the requirements of the report within the time constraints imposed by the budget that is available? If not, he should communicate that to the solicitors sooner rather than later. If the court has limited the cost of his report (and one should note at this point that the courts tend to be more forgiving of expert's fees than they are of those of the lawyers) the expert can, of course, write to the court, explaining why the fee might be insufficient and seeking guidance from the court. In the case of a unilateral instruction, the problem is for the solicitor who cannot recover the entire fee from the other side and thus has to make up the shortfall in some way, but in the case of a joint instruction, the court will have considered the appropriate fee and made an order in that regard. If the expert concludes that he cannot do the work required for the fee which has been allowed he can either decline instruction, accept the instruction on the figure which has been allowed, or query the figure with the court.

Single Joint Instruction
For the most part, the same points apply. There are some additional issues which are worth considering.

There should either be an agreed letter of instruction from both parties, in which case it should say so and there should be written confirmation from both parties that they agree to its contents. If one party writes in separate terms, that letter should be sent to the other instructing party. There can be no privileged communications in such circumstances.

Equally, in the case of a single joint instruction, if there are queries, they should be sent to both instructing parties, not just one, even if the query only applies to that side of the case. If a piece of evidence is missing, and only one side can hold it, the request can be sent to that party, but mention should be made to the other. Importantly, the expert can ask the court for guidance

On the question of the expert's view of the points on which he is asked to advise, whilst there may, once again, be a nuanced difference which is worth exploring, the parties (and the court) may appear to have completely missed the point. Whilst it is unlikely that everybody has gone off at a tangent, the expert should still raise a query. It may be that the question which he considers to be the most important has already been determined between the parties, which is why the court has limited his report to a specific issue. If there is a trite point, which the expert is not asked to consider, he should, nevertheless, state that point, albeit keeping it brief and making the point that he is not being asked to advise on that specific point. If the parties realise that they have missed something, they will ask the court for an order expanding the scope of the report.

An interesting point arises when there is a factual issue between the parties. That should be apparent on the face of the evidence put before the expert, and he should set out, and deal with the consequences of, both potential versions of events. Indeed, he might reasonably identify other possible scenarios if he considers them probable and the versions before him to be implausible. That is not to say that the expert should go off at a tangent for the fun of it, but there will be cases where there is one obvious answer, which neither party's evidence supports. The expert, having regard to CPR35 and the need to set out the range of opinion, should not be constrained to the implausible and partisan positions of the parties if there is a more compelling conclusion within the range of opinion. The expert should, however, make it clear that this third hypothesis is only raised because it is a clear and obvious conclusion having regard to the range of opinion, and he should not ignore the alternative scenarios posed by the parties. A conclusion along the lines of: "*The claimant says X, whilst the defendant says Y. The range of opinion extends from X to Y to Z, albeit that neither party asserts that Z is the case. In my experience, Z is, in fact, the most common answer in this sort of scenario, and there is no obvious reason on the evidence before me as to why that should not be the case here. Were I simply asked which of the various answers was most likely, I would say Z, because ... but if I were constrained to decide between X and Y, then I would say ... because...*"

Importantly, a single joint expert should bear in mind that there might be factual findings required as conditions precedent to his opinion being finalised. He should not be afraid to say so, and offer alternative scenarios to the court: *If A, then the answer is this. If B, then I would reach this conclusion. The issue is whether such a condition has been ful-*

filled [and the court would have to be satisfied that …]. That way, his report will assist the parties and assist the court. He might still be required to attend trial because the precise factual matrix might be nuanced and require his further input, but if the question is black or white, he will have done his job efficiently and to the satisfaction of the parties.

Finally, on the question of the expert's fees, as set out in the Protocol (see above) the parties are jointly and severally liable for the expert's fees, but the normal rule is that the parties will each pay half of the fee in the first instance, with the cost of the report becoming part of the winning party's costs. In the case of Qualified One Way Cost Shifting cases, the half that the defendant contributes to the report will not be recovered from the claimant unless the exceptions apply. Theoretically, the court might consider an order that one side or the other pay the costs of the expert in the first instance, but that would have to turn on the facts of the particular case.

In *James v MANCAT*[2] the claimant, a litigant in person, asserted that she had been the victim of discrimination because of her Obsessive Compulsive Disorder, which she averred was a disability for the purposes of the Disability Discrimination Act 1995. The defendant made no admissions as to whether the claimant did, in fact, suffer Obsessive Compulsive Disorder, or whether that constituted a disability. The Deputy District Judge ordered that a single joint expert in the field of psychiatry be instructed to opine on those two questions, but noting that the claimant was not in a position to fund that report, ordered that the defendant pay for it. The defendant appealed on the basis that the court had failed to have regard to the fact that there was no real prospect of the claimant ever paying her share of the report, because if the defendant succeeded at trial, it would struggle to recover her costs and they would, in effect, be paying for the claimant to obtain the diagnosis which she had been seeking for some time. The Circuit Judge agreed and ordered that the parties each pay 50% towards the cost of the report, failing which the action would be stayed. One suspects that the action did not proceed.

---

2   HHJ Armitage QC, Manchester County Court, 3 March 2009, unreported

CHAPTER EIGHT
SACKING AN EXPERT

There are, of course, occasions when a party to litigation does not like the answer that their expert gives. That is inevitable. In many cases, the complaint will simply be that they do not consider the expert to be sufficiently sympathetic, or over-sympathetic, to their cause. The expert, of course, would respond that they have had regard to their CPR35 duties and have formed an honest opinion having regard to all the evidence, but what about the case where there is something about the evidence which really does not sit well? The expert might have strayed outside their remit. There might have been a misunderstanding about the factual matrix which has coloured their opinion, such that when the claimant (and it's normally the claimant) corrects them, the response is unsympathetic, because the expert doubts the veracity of evidence which tends to undermine their understanding of the case. Sometimes, the opinion is fatal to the case and needs to be reviewed if the matter is to continue. Occasionally, evidence of wrongdoing on the part of the expert might leave the instructing party no choice but to look elsewhere, simply because he has lost all credibility. Equally, a resounding defeat in court on the same point with the same expert on the other side might lead a party to lose faith in their expert.

Clearly, it is manifestly unjust to saddle a party with an expert where there is a complete breakdown in the relationship between them, but equally the court, with its duty to limit expert evidence and an eye to proportionality, is not going to give a party carte blanche to shop around for an expert who happens to support its position. Given that the court's permission is required to rely on any expert, how should the court approach the situation where a party wants to change horses?

In *Edwards-Tubbs v JD Wetherspoon PLC*[1] the defendant admitted liability in respect of an accident at work in October 2005. The claimant obtained a report from an orthopaedic surgeon, a Mr Jackson, who was one of the three experts proposed under the Pre-Action Protocol. Mr Jackson examined the claimant on 19 March 2007 and reported on 14

May 2007. The claimant chose not to disclose that report and, instead, served a report from a different (and non-nominated) orthopaedic surgeon, Mr Khan, who examined the claimant on 14 July 2008 and reported the same day. That report made mention that the claimant had previously seen an orthopaedic surgeon for the purposes of a medico-legal consultation. The defendant correctly surmised that the claimant had obtained two reports and that that of Mr Jackson would be less favourable to the claimant than that of Mr Khan.

The report of Mr Jackson was, of course, privileged, so they could not demand disclosure as of right, but because the claimant required permission to rely on the report of Mr Khan, the defendant asked the court for an order that that permission be conditional upon the claimant disclosing the original report. The Deputy District Judge agreed, the Circuit Judge held that that impermissibly overrode privilege and the matter came before the Court of Appeal at the defendant's behest. It was accepted by the claimant that there was a power to impose conditions on a case management decision, at least when the change in experts came in the course of litigation, but argued that privilege attached to the pre-action report of Mr Jackson.

The Court of Appeal considered a series of authorities which had skirted around the issue, but had not gone to the heart of whether disclosure of an otherwise privileged report might be imposed as a condition to reliance upon a second expert. *Carlson v Townsend*[2] dealt with the argument as to whether a defendant's agreement to a proposed expert rendered him jointly instructed (it doesn't) and/or whether the first report was privileged. *Beck v Ministry of Defence*[3] considered whether a defendant's application for the claimant to be examined by a second psychiatrist, having lost confidence in their first instruction, should be allowed (the claim being stayed unless the claimant attended the second examination). The Court of Appeal took the view that the defendant was not obliged to disclose the report in advance of seeking permission for an examination by the second doctor (the case management order simply referred to 'a Psychiatrist') but the defendant needed

2   [2001] EWCA Civ 511

3   [2003] EWCA Civ 1043

the court's permission to have the claimant examined a second time and, for that, a condition that the first report be disclosed was appropriate. The basis for that was that an examination of a claimant needs to be justified as necessary. If it is necessary, and the claimant refuses, the action can be stayed. The claimant ought to know why he is being re-examined by a different expert, and if the defendant is being accommodated in that regard, the price is disclosure of the first report. It is, in effect, a check on the need for a second report. Finally, the case of *Haji-georgiou v Vasiliou*[4] considered (*obiter*) whether privilege overrode the court's desire to make disclosure of the abandoned report a condition precedent for reliance on the second. The court made it clear that where there was a power to attach such a condition, it should attach it.

Accordingly, in *Edwards-Tubbs*, the court took the view that whether the change in expert was pre- or post-issue, it would be appropriate for disclosure of the first report to be a condition for reliance upon the second. There is, however, an important point made: This would not apply to the scenario there a party has elected to take advice, pre-protocol, at his own expense, to assess the validity of his claim. There, the privilege would still attac.[5] The argument would be that the expert consulted at that time was not giving his opinion 'for the purposes of pr ceedings' (per *CPR*35.2).

There are, however, a series of conduct points which might arise in these cases. The reality is that a claimant is likely to know when the defendant wants to change expert for the reasons explored in *Beck*, so the more likely scenario applies where it is the claimant who wants a new expert. If the expert has already been disclosed, then clearly the defendant knows about his evidence already. Equally, if the defendant agrees to a proposed expert, only for a different expert's report to be disclosed, the defendant might well reason (as in *Carlson*) that something is amiss. The claimant might give the game away accidentally (e.g. by reference to the abandoned expert's name on a Form H, or by reference within the second report). Each of those would reasonably put the defendant on notice.

---

4   [2005] EWCA Civ 236

5   Paragraph 31

The defendant might simply ask, in any given case, whether the claimant has been medico-legally examined by any other doctor other than the reporting medic. The claimant's solicitor could not simply lie and deny the first examination, which would render that report potentially disclosable.

One problem which occasionally occurs is when a claimant, who might have been examined shortly post-accident at the behest of his then solicitors moves his instructions to another firm, only for there to be difficulties in securing the file from the first solicitors. That should not, of course, happen, but there are risks that the claimant might lay himself open to disclosure of a report which is not in his possession, the contents of which he cannot recall.

The way around these problems is, in all likelihood, simply to embrace the fact that there are two conflicting reports, and to get the second expert to explain why the first one is wrong, in much the same way as one might approach the report obtained by the other side. CPR35.11 provides that: *"Where a party has disclosed an experts' report, any party may use that expert's report as evidence at the trial."* If there is a cogent reason for showing that the first expert is wrong, and the expert being relied upon has debunked the first report, the other side might need to apply to call the expert at trial, but that is unlikely to happen if they have their own expert already (because there would then be three), and if they don't have their own expert, would they really want to go with the claimant's first choice rather than seek their own? That would be a decision for the case management judge.

The situation might arise where the disclosing party might still have good reason for wanting the initial expert to attend trial for cross-examination. Again, that would be a matter for the case management judge, but could well arise if the alternative was to grant an unfair tactical advantage (e.g. if the defendant wanted to rely upon the claimant's first expert and adopt his report).

The reality of the situation is probably more prosaic. If you have already paid for an expert's report, but don't like it, in what circumstances is a party likely to want to invest a further sum to obtain a second report? It is unlikely to be the case in claims of modest value, unless the factual basis of the report is wholly at odds with the claimant's instructions. The more likely scenario is that the problem will arise in potentially valuable litigation where there is more at stake, and the court will have to decide what evidence, pursuant to CPR35.1, is reasonably required. If that means that a party who loses faith in his first expert wants to abandon the monies spent on that expert (and potentially all costs thrown away on the other side), the potential gain has to justify that expense. The later that decision comes in the litigation, the more costly that will be.

PART TWO

THE PRESENTATION OF EVIDENCE

Having considered how one goes about obtaining an expert report, it is worth considering the requirements of such a report, both formal, as set out in CPR35 and the Practice Direction, and substantive, which is, of course, the import of the report. In this part, we consider the drafting of the report and the reporting process in general terms, amendments to, and clarification of, an expert's opinion both before and after service, either after conference or CPR35 questions, joint reports and the giving of evidence at trial if required.

Whilst Part One was primarily for the benefit of those seeking to instruct experts, this Part is aimed at both experts and those instructing them. For the former, it is hoped that rendering express the thought processes which, for many, are functions of their subconscious might allow a clarity of thought and expression which makes their opinion more useful. For the latter, understanding what one might hope to achieve with an expert's report will allow those reading them to identify any potential lacunae or failings with a view to correcting them, or at last realising the problem, in good time.

CHAPTER NINE
THE FORMALITIES

The requirements of form and content of an expert's report are set out in paragraph 3 of the Practice Direction to CPR35 and are some of the most misunderstood provisions of CPR. These matters go to both form **and** content, and the mere fact that the report contains the relevant words is all too often a matter of form only.

3.1 An expert's report should be addressed to the court and not to the party from whom the expert has received instructions. This was, of course, one of the central tenets of the Civil Procedure Rules 1997. The days of hired gun experts were to be put behind us. All experts would comply with the Practice Direction and there would be no need for two experts of the same discipline in a case, or so it was suggested.

The reality is that practically every report that one reads complies with this requirement simply by writing the words: "To the court" on the front page, as if that suffices. It does not. It might provide the expert with a reminder that his report is to be used for the purposes of litigation rather than merely be an advisory piece, but that is not the purpose of this requirement. The report is provided to the court, and the expert's duty is to the court, because what is required of the expert is for him to utilise his expertise, in compliance with the requirements of the Practice Direction and particularly paragraph 3.2(6) thereof (see below). One might speculate that because experts give oral evidence far less than they did 20 years ago, they have forgotten how Judges might respond to partisan opinions or inadequacy of reporting. The excuse for not calling an expert is often that it is not cost-effective, but if the same mistakes are made over and over again, how might one control the experts? The answer is that this requirement of addressing the court must be taken at face value and enforced.

3.2 An expert's report must:
(1) give details of the expert's qualifications;
This really should not be very difficult, but there is a tendency, once again, to comply the requirement in terms of form, rather than content.

Stating that one is MBChB DFFP is all very interesting, but actually explaining that you hold a Bachelor's Degree in Medicine and Surgery, and a Diploma in Family Planning, is slightly more relevant if you're giving evidence in respect of the contraceptive advice given by a GP. The rule should be read as requiring the expert to justify his status as an expert, not whether or not he took his French GCSE a year early (also a qualification). This is particularly true in the case of membership of trade organisations. Is that a qualification? It depends to some extent on what that trade organisation actually does. Does it require any sort of application other than payment of a fee? Does it offer training or objective standards? What is the commitment required to attain and retain that membership?

The simplest way for an expert to state his qualifications and thus comply with the form of this rule is to attach his CV, even if only a potted version, to his report, but to comply with the requirement in terms of content, the wise expert might consider a 3 or 4 line explanation of what he actually does and why he should be taken as an expert in such matters.

(2) give details of any literature or other material which has been relied on in making the report;
(3) contain a statement setting out the substance of all facts and instructions which are material to the opinions expressed in the report or upon which those opinions are based;
(4) make clear which of the facts stated in the report are within the expert's own knowledge;

These 3 requirements are grouped together because, whether specific information is within the expert's own knowledge or is a fact which he has extracted from his instructions, or information from a previously published paper, there is a real expectation that the expert will adopt a transparent and scientific approach, disclosing the basis for the opinion that he has formed. If he does not, what, if anything, can one read into his report?

This really should not be very difficult. In the cases of generic soft tissue injury reports, there will be certain core papers which should have been considered by the expert before starting to write such reports. In the case of esoteric injuries where true specialism is required, one would expect the expert either to have written papers on the subject and/or be au fait with the leading authorities on the topic. It is not, however, limited to technical papers. In the case of engineers, they will need to look at British Standards, papers provided by RoSPA and similar documentation.

One point of particular relevance for engineers in NIHL cases is the extent to which they can rely on their previous experience of similar types of work and the likely noise levels produced. The difficulty for the litigants in such cases, as set out elsewhere, is that there is an exchange of the evidence available in the instant case, and the engineer is then invited to opine, leading some experts to assert that they do not have sufficient information to conclude that noise levels were excessive. Should they, in those circumstances, opine based on their knowledge from other cases? To some extent, they do already, because they are bringing their understanding and background knowledge into play by dint of their status as experts. The difficulty comes when they cannot back up the basis of that knowledge by documentation. In the event of two separate experts, there can be challenges to such conclusions, but with a single joint expert (as normally happens in that particular circumstance) one is simply left with the expert saying: "Because I say so." It is all the more important in those cases that the documentation and other material relied upon is set out on the face of the report so that it can be disclosed and studied by the parties.

It is also worth noting that any document referred to by the expert on the face of the report is, in effect, disclosed. A party cannot send a document to the expert without the expectation that it will be disclosed to the other side, and in the case of pre-action reports, that potentially leads to an early exchange of witness statements. The party wanting to avoid being put at a disadvantage in that regard should press for mutual early exchange.

There is an important point which relates to soft tissue injury reports. It is the practice of many reporting experts to ask clients to complete ques-

tionnaires whilst they are waiting for the appointments as it allows a
stream-lining of the process. Such a document is arguably within
35PD.3.6(2) as 'material'. Given how often such reports are challenged
on the basis of minor discrepancies, or arguments arise about the wording of the question pertaining to pre-accident history, one often sees
requests for disclosure of that questionnaire to confirm what was actually said. Often it is averred that the document has been destroyed,
which is hard to believe – this is clearly a relevant step to the production
of the report. Indeed, if an expert is going to use this method, there is a
strong argument that it should be annexed to the report as an
Appendix.

*(5) say who carried out any examination, measurement, test or experiment
which the expert has used for the report, give the qualifications of that person, and say whether or not the test or experiment has been carried out
under the expert's supervision;*
This is commonly seen in Noise Induced Hearing Loss claims, where
the audiogram is taken by somebody other than the Consultant; in
Accident Reconstruction claims, where measurements are taken by, or
in association with, an assistant to the expert; and Damage Consistency
reports where the opining expert might be working from photographs
taken by another. The logic to the rule is obvious – the origin of the
evidence upon which the expert bases his opinion should be transparent. As a matter of good practice, if the investigation is carried out by
somebody other than the expert, he should explain why that was necessary.

*(6) where there is a range of opinion on the matters dealt with in the report
–*

(a) summarise the range of opinions; and
(b) give reasons for the expert's own opinion;
This is arguably the single most ignored and/or misunderstood requirement of the Civil Procedure Rules and is dealt with in more detail in
the next Chapter. It is the core principle of CPR35. Were the courts to
enforce it, it would change the landscape of civil litigation.

(7) contain a summary of the conclusions reached;

This is a straight-forward requirement, designed to focus the mind of the expert and assist both the parties and the court, rather than requiring a detailed analysis of a rambling narrative. The conclusion can be set out at the start of the report, or the end, although in the latter case it tends to follow on directly from the discussion and opinion sections of the report. Writing a lengthy analysis and then a short summary immediately afterwards is counterintuitive for many, and as a matter of good practice it is worth bringing the summary of conclusions forwards to the start of the report before explaining the reasons in more detail.

(8) if the expert is not able to give an opinion without qualification, state the qualification;

One often sees an expert saying that they need further information before giving a final opinion. In medical reports, the results of updated scans or X-rays are an integral part of assessing the current state of the injury and the progression of any deterioration. There are, however, other qualifications which the careful expert should consider in his report. In cases involving soft tissue injuries, he should at least acknowledge that he is dependent on the veracity of the claimant and/or the accuracy of the history presented. That is one of most commonly asked Part 35 questions in such a case and there is no reason why the expert should not deal with it at the first time of asking, rather than waiting to be prompted. If he does his job properly, he can assess the credibility of the patient as he examines and explain why he accepts (or doesn't) their credibility. Simply saying: "I found them credible" is not enough, particularly in cases where the expert is unilaterally instructed. Credibility is ultimately a matter for the court, but testing which tends to support the consistency of a complaint is appropriate and should be referred to in the report.

(9) contain a statement that the expert –
(a) understands their duty to the court, and has complied with that duty; and
(b) is aware of the requirements of Part 35, this practice direction and the Guidance for the Instruction of Experts in Civil Claims 2014.

This requirement exemplifies the difference between form and content. Every report contains these words or some reference to them, because it can form part of the standard template of a report, but that is not to say that the expert actually understands them. If he did, he would set out the range of opinion and comply with 35PD.3(6), rather than paying lip service to it. Many experts give the impression that they fulfil this requirement by acknowledging that their duty *is* to the court, rather than showing that they understand the *nature* of their duty to the court. That failing then effects their non-compliance with other aspects of the Practice Direction and affects the whole report.

3.3 An expert's report must be verified by a statement of truth in the following form –
I confirm that I have made clear which facts and matters referred to in this report are within my own knowledge and which are not. Those that are within my own knowledge I confirm to be true. The opinions I have expressed represent my true and complete professional opinions on the matters to which they refer.

The statement of truth on an expert's report is not the same as the statement of truth on a witness statement, but the effects are. Appending a statement of truth, knowing that the contents of the report are not true, is a contempt of court. Experts, because they rarely go to court, and because they tend to be treated with respect when they do attend, are rarely challenged on this, but the reality is that unless they have set out the range of opinion and their reasons for their position, they cannot *show* that they have set out their complete professional opinions. It is a matter of showing one's working. An instructing party should try to protect its expert if a draft report does not deal with all of the requirements of PD35 by ensuring that the report is complete before service. That job will fall to the lawyer, rather than the client, and the lawyer should be alert to the potential failings of the expert at all stages. If the expert needs to rethink the style, structure or content of his reports to comply with the rules, then he simply needs to get on with it. The reality is that unless the courts are prepared to take a hard line and disallow the fees of experts who do not comply with CPR35, they will continue to fail in their duties to the court.

That said, the expert who fails to comply with his duties is no longer immune from suit. The case of *Jones v Kaney*[1] saw the Supreme Court conclude by a majority (5:2) that expert witnesses were not immune from claims in tort or contract for matters connected with their participation in legal proceedings. In that case the claimant's expert, a consultant clinical psychologist, originally expressed the view that the claimant was suffering from post traumatic stress disorder whilst the defendant's insurers took the view that the claimant was exaggerating. At the joint report stage, a number of concessions were made with the expert (K) concluding that the claimant has been 'very deceptive and deceitful in his reporting' and concluded that he had only suffered an adjustment disorder. On an application to strike out the claimant's claim against his former expert before a Defence was filed, the Supreme Court ruled that there was no immunity. Lord Brown suggested that it may be that the most likely consequence of the removal of experts' immunity from suit will be "*a sharpened awareness of the risks of pitching their initial views of the merits of their client's case too high or too inflexibly*".

Whilst the impression from *Jones v Kaney* is that the expert may well have reached the correct answer in the end, one can only imagine that getting it right in the first instance might have saved everybody time and money.

---

1   [2011] UKSC 13

CHAPTER TEN
THE RANGE OF OPINION

As school children, we are encouraged, particularly in mathematics, to show our working. Marks are awarded for it, and the reason for that is simple – stating a conclusion without backing it up and explaining how one reaches that point makes it impossible to assess its validity. It is all too easy for an 'expert' to proffer an opinion (we see it on a daily basis in the media) but what the court actually wants from an expert is evidence, because it is evidence which forms the foundations of findings of fact, which allow the court to determine cases. A bare assertion that something is the case might as well be written on water.

When the Civil Procedure Rules were first introduced, one of the fundamental and radical ideas was that there would be one expert in any given discipline and that he would be the court's expert, rather than one particular party's. Before CPR, both sides would habitually instruct an expert, one would say X, the other would say Y, they would both come to court, the judge would hear their evidence and decide which one he preferred. This was deemed to be expensive, and a potential drain on the time of the experts. It also meant that trials had to be listed months in advance to ensure that the experts would be available. The purpose of CPR was expedite matters, and one way of doing that was to reduce the number of times that experts would have to attend court by making sure that their evidence was, insofar as possible, dealt with on paper.

With that in mind, the experts were told that, in order to fulfil their duty to the court, they had to set out the range of opinion as an integral part of their report. The reasons are obvious: if an expert is actually going to explain to the court why he has come to conclusion A, he needs to say what conclusions are available to him. To simply give one's conclusion is to deny the possibility of a different point of view, and given that expert evidence is, by its very nature, one of opinion, the evidence would have to be both objective and compelling to allow anybody to reject all possible alternatives. Clearly, there are cases where there is only one conclusion: The mathematical calculation[1], or the scientific experiment which disproves putative alternatives, are examples. In a medical context, an amputated finger is unlikely to grow back. The idea, however, of only one conclusion is fundamentally implausible in the case of a more nuanced question, such as the likely recovery time from an injury. One might opine as to the most likely answer, but that is not the same thing.

For that reason, the range of opinion is a crucial part of any expert's report. By setting out that range, even if some of the points within that range are obvious, or even ridiculous, the court, the parties, any opposing expert and the writer of the report himself can assess whether the foundations for his conclusions are valid. As a matter of good practice, an expert should stop and think about those aspects of his process, each and every time, to ensure that he is doing a proper job, irrespective of any express duty to the court. For many, the questions become second nature, but that is not to say that they are sacrosanct. Indeed, it is the failure to reassess the norms which causes people to fall into error.

It is not a complicated process: it is normally a simple stepping back from the data immediately available and asking why that data is being considered in the first place. Identifying the totality of that data and the reasons for the analysis allows the writer of a report to set out the basis for his opinion so that he might justify himself when challenged. He is, as Archimedes recommended, looking for a place to stand.

So what is the range of opinion? It depends, of course, on the speciality of the expert and the facts of the case upon which he is opining, and that is why it is so important that the range of opinion is set out on the face of the report. Later chapters deal with specific types of expert and the range of opinion in any given case, but it is worth identifying what factors should be considered.

---

1 Assuming that the data can be confirmed to be accurate. Often the expert has to opine on the basis of limited data and, rightly, has to speculate as to the tolerance one might allow in respect of measurements and the like.

In the case of, say, engineers, the range tends to arise because there are uncertainties in the initial data, so that the conclusions are inevitably being drawn from non-absolute 'facts'. The assessment of the accuracy of the data, and the range of values which might be assigned, is a judgment call which is properly the remit of the expert. It might be the case that detailed measurements were taken at the scene of the accident which allow the expert to rely on the data. He might need to undertake his own testing, using his knowledge and expertise of the questions to be asked and the methods by which data might be gathered, to opine as to the base facts so that he might draw conclusions from them in due course.

For doctors, there is an uncertainty inherent in relying upon the complaints of symptoms, particularly in the context of litigation, and part of the skillset is in determining the validity of those complaints. The crux of the formation of the doctor's opinion is more fundamental.

The Pendulum

For many years, I have put forward a simple analysis of the range of opinion in medico-legal cases:

The range of medico-legal opinion in any given case must have three extreme points:
(a) That the claimant has all of the symptoms of which he complains and that they are all caused by the accident;
(b) That the claimant has all of the symptoms of which he complains, but none of them is caused by the accident;
(c) That the claimant has none of the symptoms of which he complains.

Were one to suspend a pendulum from a tripod, its feet positioned at those extremes, the pendulum, like the expert's opinion, must come to rest somewhere in the triangle created.

That is not to say that the pendulum must fall at one of those three extremes – it is just as likely to fall somewhere in the middle, with some of the symptoms being constitutional, some being slightly over-stated, and some being down to the accident. The import of this analysis is this: if one is reporting for a claimant, in the same way as one might treat a patient in a non-litigation scenario, the tendency is to accept their complaints as *prima facie* real. In a treating context, one can do no other, because to ignore a complaint without investigation and/or good reason is to invite disaster. For doctors who habitually treat patients, or for those who habitually report for claimants, it is difficult to put aside that mindset and assess with absolute objectivity. The Pendulum allows, indeed insists on, a contemplation and assessment of the alternatives.

If, after due consideration, one of those extremes can be rejected, or the opinion starts to take shape towards one specific conclusion, then by evidencing that thought process and giving reasons for the opinion being expressed, the expert's credibility can only ever be enhanced. The common complaint about experts reporting for claimants is that they are too generous. The common complaint about experts reporting for defendants is that they are too mean. Those perceptions are just as partisan and polarised as the perceived underlying bias of the experts – the claimant might accept that his expert has been a little sympathetic towards him, but is rarely going to acknowledge that the opinion expressed is overly so. By setting out the reasons for rejecting the alternatives, the expert strengthens his own position by identifying the weaknesses in the alternatives. For that reason, 35PD.3.2(6) is crucial to any expert's report.

Many (if not most) experts, however, fail to engage with this analysis. Saying: "In my opinion, the claimant will recover within 10-12 months" is not giving the range of opinion (which, logically, extends from "The claimant was not injured" to "The claimant will never recover"). It is simply stating a figure. Whether that is even a genuine opinion is hard to discern, because the expert has rarely set out any other information to suggest that the opinion that he has given is his "true and complete" opinion.

The difficulty is that the court rarely has the time or inclination to assess the credibility of that opinion, particularly in the context of low value, soft tissue injury, claims. The expert says *x* months of symptoms, the claimant confirms that, lo, the expert was correct, and the court assesses damages. On a number of occasions, I have asked the question: "What percentage of patients come back, complaining that they have not, in fact, recovered within the proposed timescale?" The majority concede figures of less than 1%. That, with respect to those experts, suggests that there is something wrong with the opinions that they express. If, however, they identified the range of opinion and their reasons for rejecting the alternatives, it would be far harder to challenge their evidence. At that point, the purpose of CPR35 might, in fact, be fulfilled.

So what should the court do? The current mindset does not contemplate, save in individual cases, the possibility of challenging the opinions of an expert, and the costs and practicalities of a test case to determine whether a particular expert's opinions are right or wrong are sufficiently off-putting, particularly when set against the fact that no precedent would be created, to dissuade that course. One possibility is for litigants to challenge the validity of the report, when first served, identifying the breaches of CPR35, and requiring the expert to comply with the requirements, but the questioning party is still liable to pay the costs of answering those questions. Another is to seek to persuade the court to make an order that the expert answer those specific questions without getting paid for his answers, on the basis that had he complied with the Practice Direction, he would have answered the questions within the first report for the same price as he has been paid. To do that, however, requires the matter to come before the court, so that the order can be made. Alternatively, one might simply reject any report which does not comply with the Practice Direction and require the matter to be litigated, but that is potentially expensive in the short term. There is no easy answer to the problem, but a change in mindset is required, failing which PD35.2(6) will continue to be ignored and the fundamental premise of CPR35 will be rendered (or, more accurately, will remain) impotent.

CHAPTER ELEVEN
MANIPULATING EXPERT
EVIDENCE

When an expert has provided a report, the instructing party and/or the opposing party might wish to challenge it. It might not go far enough. It might be internally inconsistent. It might, simply, reach a conclusion which is unacceptable to one or other party.

The instructing party

Assuming unilateral instruction, the party instructing an expert has a degree of control over the release of the report. If the report is unfavourable to the case, it is unlikely to see the light of day, and the party will have to decide whether to seek a second opinion. In those cases, as Chapter 8 shows, issues might arise as to whether the court imposes a condition precedent to reliance upon the second report, by way of an order that privilege is waived in respect of the original.

There will be cases where the party reads the report which has been produced and identifies factual errors. Those might be relevant to the expert's opinion, and if changes are to be suggested to the expert (e.g. where in the car the claimant was sitting), he should be invited to consider whether that will change his opinions. Those matters are relatively straight-forward, although there is always the chance that the other side will ask whether the report disclosed is a first draft.

Equally, there will be cases where there is further information which the expert might reasonably need to consider before finalising his views. In cases where that information should have been available to the expert at the time of his writing his report, it can jar if a second report is prepared making reference to something which should have been in the original. If, on the other hand, the evidence has been obtained in response to the first report, it makes much more sense for the information to be included in an addendum. Test results or scans fall into this category, and there will be occasions where the medical records are required before a final opinion is given. In that case, there is little stylistic difference between an amended report which says: "Having interviewed the claimant, I asked to see his A&E records and have been provided with them" and a second report which is an addendum setting out the findings and confirming (or altering) the view originally expressed. One occasionally sees a second report which is, in effect, the first report with a separate section tagged on to the end, dealing with the further information. Whilst helpful in the sense that it is only one document, it is imperative that the expert makes it clear that the first section is unaltered, and clarifies which information is new.

If it simply a case of providing the expert with further information, the obvious and transparent way in which to do so is in writing. Those further instructions can be disclosed to the receiving party as required.

The more difficult question arises when the instructing party, upon receipt of the report, takes the view that either the emphasis is wrong, or the conclusions of the expert need to be tested.

Often, in those cases, the instructing party appreciates when the expert is instructed that the case is potentially difficult. Sometimes the potential issues only arise when the report is received. In either event, it is undoubtedly helpful to produce a draft report (i.e. not one for the purposes of litigation) in the first instance and then to have a conference with the expert. It may be that the report is then amended without specific additional information being provided, simply because the discussion has opened up other areas of consideration, or has clarified the views of the expert. That report is then prepared 'for the purposes of proceedings' and falls within CPR35. The report, and communications with the expert, are covered by privilege until disclosed.

There will be circumstances where the conference gives rise to specific new issues, not contained in the first report. It is then a matter for the instructing party and the expert to decide whether a further formal letter should be sent, identifying those further issues by way of formal instruction, or questions, to allow the expert to answer them *de novo* or whether simply to include them in the CPR35 report. If the issue can be raised in a single, neat, question then that may be preferable, in that it acknowledges that the expert has been asked a question to clarify his views and has shown a degree of flexibility and willingness to consider new issues as and when they arise, suggesting that he understands and appreciates his CPR35 duties.

The receiving party
From the receiving party's perspective, the mechanism for challenging the report in the first instance is the asking of questions pursuant to CPR35.6, which provides that:

(1) A party may put written questions about an expert's report (which must be proportionate) to –
(a) an expert instructed by another party; or
(b) a single joint expert appointed under rule 35.7.

The requirement of proportionality runs throughout the Civil Procedure Rules, and it is no surprise that it appears here, although it does presuppose that the expert has produced a report which is CPR35 compliant in the first place. Given the requirements of CPR35.6(2)(c), set out below, and the requirement that the report sets out the expert's complete professional opinion, one can understand how the rule makers might consider that questions should be proportionate. After all, if a complete professional opinion has been provided which sets out the range of opinion and the reasons for adopting a position within that range, and one is only seeking clarification, how complicated and disproportionate can one be? If, however, the report does not do its job at the first time of asking, it is hard to see how a question designed to clarify the opinion so that it complies with CPR35 could be said to be disproportionate.

(2) Written questions under paragraph (1) –
(a) may be put once only;
(b) must be put within 28 days of service of the expert's report; and
(c) must be for the purpose only of clarification of the report,
unless in any case –
(I) the court gives permission; or
(ii) the other party agrees.

The limitations on the nature of written questions are well known to litigators, who are often keen to protect their experts from repeated questioning and attempts to undermine their credibility, but the exception that the court can give permission for questions which go beyond the limitations of the primary rule is often underestimated, particularly in respect of (c). The asking of a second set of questions, particularly if they arise from the answer to the first set of questions, or represent a discrete but easily dealt with point, is hardly likely to be disproportionate. The asking of questions after 28 days of service is almost inevitably allowed, because the case management order normally gives permission for CPR35 questions as part of the standard directions in the case, even though the report was almost certainly served pre-proceedings and again with the Claim Form.

The real issue here as to whether the court will permit questions which go beyond mere clarification of the report. The primary purpose of CPR35 questions is not to cross-examine the expert as to his *bona fides* or competence, and it is hard to see how those might constitute clarification, but if the questioning party can identify a real issue with the expert and the way in which he forms his opinion in a given case, the court may well give permission to ask questions that go beyond mere clarification. The most appropriate method would be to raise the issue on the face of the Defence, identifying the perceived flaws, and draft the questions (if possible) in advance of directions, so that they might be submitted to the court for approval at the case management stage.

There is an important point to the provisions of subsections (1) and (2). Paragraph 6.2 of the Practice Direction to CPR35 provides that the party or parties instructing an expert must pay the expert's fees for answering those questions, albeit that this does not affect any decision of the court as to the party who is ultimately to bear those costs.

The apparent purpose of that provision is to render certainty as to the expert's remuneration. He should know who is going to pay him for his work, and the rules make it clear that the instructing party is under that obligation. That said, 35PD.6.2 makes it clear that the court has the ultimate discretion as to who might pay.

Clearly, if the CPR35 questions are justified, because the report needs clarification, there will be no need for the court to consider any sort of specific costs provision in respect of the expert's response, but if and to the extent that the asking party is straying beyond the traditional limits of CPR35.6, either because the questions go beyond mere clarification or are a second set of questions, the court might consider ordering that the asking party pay those costs in any event. There is no reason why those costs should be deferred to the end of the case either. Against that, if the reason for the questions is the expert's failure to address something which was identified by the asking party as relevant before the report was produced, the asking party might well ask the court, in allowing its questions, for an order that the instructing party is liable for those costs in any event. The court would need to see the questions in advance and the various points set out above would have to be considered. The most likely scenario would be where the instructing party objected to the extent or the nature of the questions at the case management hearing and the court had to consider the reasonableness of the parties' respective conduct.

(3) An expert's answers to questions put in accordance with paragraph (1) shall be treated as part of the expert's report.
This appears to be relatively obvious proposition, but becomes relevant if, for instance, the instructing party thereafter loses faith in the expert and instructs an alternative and the questioning party wishes to rely upon the totality of his evidence.

(4) Where –
(a) a party has put a written question to an expert instructed by another party; and
(b) the expert does not answer that question,
the court may make one or both of the following orders in relation to the party who instructed the expert –
(I) that the party may not rely on the evidence of that expert; or
(ii) that the party may not recover the fees and expenses of that expert from any other party.

There has to be a sanction available to the court in the event that an expert does not comply with the requirement to answer the questions. The alternative sanctions suggested (and they are not mandatory) recognise that the fault for the failure might lie with the party, or the expert, or simply circumstance. If an expert, having reported, ceases to practice, or dies, it would hardly be just to penalise the instructing party because he cannot answer a specific question, nor might it be proportionate to instruct a new expert, depending on the issue to which the evidence goes. If, on the other hand, there is evidence that the failure to comply is deliberate and unjustified, one or both of the suggested penalties might persuade the expert to assist the court.

The purpose of CPR35 questions is therefore to identify, to the satisfaction of the questioning party and/or the court, the validity of the expert's opinion. In certain cases, the questions will be aimed at setting up a question of fact for the court to determine, which would then trigger one or other of the expert's stated opinions in a manner which would be dispositive.

If and to the extent that the questioning party is dissatisfied with the responses from an expert, it can apply to ask further questions, ask to cross-examine the expert at trial, or seek its own expert, which is dealt with in the next chapter.

CHAPTER TWELVE
MULTIPLE EXPERTS

The introduction of CPR35 was designed to instigate a shift in how expert evidence was obtained and used by the parties in any given case. CPR35.1 gave the court the power to control that evidence, CPR35.3 made it clear that the expert's duty was to the court, and CPR35.4 makes it clear that the court's permission is required before a report may be put in evidence. As already discussed, the master plan was that in any given case the reporting expert would produce a balanced, expansive report which provided the court with any and all relevant information so that the court might make an informed decision. The parties were encouraged to agree Single Joint Experts if appropriate and the Protocols were there to make sure that experts were proposed openly by the instructing party. CPR35.6 permitted proportionate questions to an opponent's expert for the purpose of clarifying the report, although the court can permit questions to go beyond that.

Often, however, one party (normally the defendant) will be unhappy with the conclusions of the claimant's expert and will seek its own evidence to counter it. The decision to allow that second report is a matter for the court and will normally be made at the case management conference or by reference to a specific application by the defendant to rely upon its own expert.

The courts clearly envisaged that the parties would, in the first instance, jump through the hoops of CPR35.6 questions before justifying the need for a second opinion by evidence identifying the defendant's dissatisfaction with the state of the evidence. In *Daniels v Walker*[1] the Court of Appeal held that where the dissatisfied party's reasons were not fanciful, the court could allow them to obtain its own expert report. If and to the extent that it would be unjust to prevent that party from relying upon that evidence (and subject to meetings of experts and the like) the party will be allowed to rely upon that evidence at trial.

---

1 [2000] 1 WLR 1382, CA

In reality, particularly with added pressure to keep costs to a proportionate level, courts have come to accept that there are some cases where CPR35.6 questions will never satisfy the defendant, will add time, cost and complexity to the case, and will ultimately require another hearing to determine the defendant's application for its own evidence. There might have been issues with the instruction of the claimant's expert in the first instance. The defendant might have identified specific issues with this specific expert in the past, such that his position (or, indeed, credibility) is untenable in their eyes. It might be the case that whilst there is no issue with the expert himself, the defendant, as a matter of policy, takes a different view. This is particularly common in cases involving allegations of Low Velocity Impact, or in cases involving questions of causation (e.g. in Noise Induced Hearing Loss claims). There might simply be an awful lot of money at stake, such that the court might feel that both sides should have their own expert.

The most common scenario, of course, distils to this: The claimant's expert is perceived, by the defendant (or the court) to have alighted on a position which is at the extreme end of (or beyond) the range of reasonable opinion.

That, of course, may have been the reason for selecting him in the first place, and if he hasn't set out the range of opinion before justifying his position within it, it tends to make it easier for the defendant to persuade the court that a more balanced view is required. Of course, that often leads to the defendant picking an expert who goes too far the other way, but that is a matter for them.

CHAPTER THIRTEEN
JOINT REPORTS

Once the court has permitted both sides to obtain their own evidence, there is the potential that they will reach different conclusions. Occasionally, those differences will be so nuanced that the parties themselves decide that no joint report is required, but CPR35.12 specifically permits the court to direct a discussion between experts of like (or similar) discipline.

The rule[1] mentions two specific purposes: (a) to identify and discuss the expert issues in the proceedings; and (b) where possible, reach an agreed opinion on those issues. The court may specify the issues which the experts must discuss.[2]

This section of the rule normally goes by the by, because the issues in the case are normally relatively clear cut, but there may be complex medical issues, perhaps with interaction between different disciplines (a classic case being the orthopaedic injury with associated psychological symptoms leading to the involvement of pain management experts) or other circumstances where the court, the parties and the experts themselves might well benefit from somebody taking a step back, considering what is, in fact, in issue between the parties and using the experts to clarify the questions to be asked before trying to answer them. This would be particularly useful to a party who felt that the other side's expert was straying away from his field of expertise, with the court using its powers to make the experts set out the issues so that one or other might set out his claim that the position that the other side is raising is actually beyond their expertise.

CPR35.12(3) permits the court to direct that, following the discussion between the experts, they should agree a statement for the court setting out those issues on which "(a) they agree; and (b) they disagree with a summary of their reasons for disagreeing." In the normal course of

---

1 CPR35.12(1)

2 CPR35.12(2)

events, once the court has directed a discussion, unless that is a preliminary discussion to decide what they might need to discuss, a joint report will inevitably follow.

The first problem with the rule is that it is rather simplistic in its wording, and without further guidance from the Court, experts often 'summarise' their reasons for disagreeing solely by restating their own respective positions, rather than actively considering the alternative viewpoint(s). The experts should, of course, having regard to their obligations to set out the range of opinion before identifying their respective positions within that range and their reasons for alighting on that position, find it easy to assess their opponent's position within the range and explain why they reject that view, or at least favour their own. Of course, if they have not set out the range of opinion in the first instance, it becomes significantly more difficult. Psychologically, if you have not already accepted the remainder of the possibilities before putting forward your conclusion, it must be difficult to accept that somebody else might actually be right, whereas if you've considered that position and can legitimately distance yourself from it by analysis, the joint report is an easier exercise.

The Court could, and, it is submitted, should, make an order which spells out the need for that methodology. It is not difficult. In an ideal world, the case management order might reasonably be along the lines of:

"By [date] the experts of like discipline shall speak and, if necessary, meet, to discuss the case and thereafter, by [date] produce a joint statement to the Court complying with the following requirements:
  1. *The experts shall identify the issues in respect of which they consider themselves able to opine within the proceedings and, in the event that they are unable to agree the same, identify which matters are outwith their respective capacity to opine and their reasons why;*
  2. *The experts shall set out the range of opinion in respect of each issue which they consider to be relevant and in respect of which they consider themselves able to opine;*

3. *The experts shall set out any agreement which they are able to reach in respect of each such issue;*

4. *In respect of any disagreement on any given issue, the experts should each identify their reasons for adopting their own position and their reasons for rejecting the alternative position."*

A simpler order might require the experts to produce a joint report setting out their reasons for disagreeing,to include their respective reasons for rejecting the alternative position, but experience suggests that without the additional requirement being identified by the Court, the joint report can end up being a list of the experts' respective views (often expressed sequentially rather than concurrently) without any real explanation as to why they differ. Certain experts are clearly better than others in this respect, and much depends on the relationship that they have with each other – one often receives disjointed joint reports only to be told by one's own, disgruntled, expert that it was the other expert's fault and that they could not engage in the writing of the report.

Certain areas of expertise engender their own problems. The joint report of the care experts is inevitably expressed as a Scott Schedule (which is helpful) but rarely is there sufficient analysis of why one set of figures is correct and the other one wrong. It would assist the Court greatly if the report could reflect the date of trial in some way, rather than each expert ending their 'past' analysis as at the date of their own report with a 'future' provision starting at some apparently random point in the past, but that pales into insignificance when the reader realises that neither side has moved from their original reports and there is no analysis of why they are right and the other side is wrong. That certainly does not assist the Court and it can only be a matter of time before a disappointed trial judge orders the experts to have another go at their own expense. A timeous case management order of the sort suggested above might serve to avoid those problems.

THE MECHANICS OF A JOINT REPORT

The reality is that the experts are unlikely to meet face to face to discuss their joint report and are more likely to conduct the discussion over the telephone, with one or other then writing up a first draft and the other adding or editing in due course.

The first point, of course, is to ensure that both experts have seen the other's report, together with any other relevant documentation (e.g. updated medical notes) in advance of that meeting. If there is a specific order as regards the meeting, or the contents of that joint report, that should also be supplied. Often, experts in one field appear oblivious to the fact that there are experts in another field engaged in a similar exercise, to whom they themselves might defer.

Secondly, whether in line with an order as suggested above, or of the experts' own volition, it is potentially useful to have a framework prepared in advance. That would allow the experts to make sure that they are, in fact, covering the ground required of them in the joint report.

Thirdly, each issue should, if possible, be dealt with separately, rather than each expert writing his half of the report. Whether the discussion on a given point requires a Scott Schedule approach will depend on the issues arising, but a simply to-ing and fro-ing in sub-paragraphs should be relatively easy to engineer along the lines of:

1. As to [issue]:
    1.1 The range of opinion is …;
    1.2 The evidence available is …;
    1.3 What is agreed:
    1.4 What is not agreed:
        1.4.1 Mr X opines that … because …;
        1.4.2 Mr Y (accepts that Mr X is within the range of opinion but) disagrees with Mr X because … and opines that … because …;

1.4.3   Mr X has considered Mr Y's opinion (and accepts that Mr Y is within the range of opinion) but rejects it because … and maintains his view.

Fourthly, if a particular factual issue falls to be determined by the court, with consequences for one or both expert opinions, that should be set out on the face of the report:

"Ultimately, the court will need to make a finding on the factual issue as to …. Were the court to find that … occurred, then Mr X would opine … and Mr Y would opine …, whilst if the court were to find that … occurred, then Messrs X and Y would agree that …".

The purpose of a joint report between the experts is not simply to draw battle lines for trial or to reach agreement. A good report will permit the parties to consider whether they actually need the experts to give live evidence at trial, even if there are apparent disagreements on the face of the joint report. Often, what appears to be a significant difference between the experts comes down to their approaching the question in different ways, or even just semantics. By following the relatively straight-forward steps set out above, that should become apparent to all of the parties well before trial.

CHAPTER FOURTEEN
LIVE EVIDENCE

In the vast majority of cases, expert evidence, having been reduced to writing in the original report and then clarified by judicious CPR35 questions and/or joint reports, stands without the need for oral cross-examination. There are, however, cases (few and far between) where experts still need to attend court. This chapter examines when it might be appropriate for experts to give live evidence and then considers the pros and cons of sequential evidence (the traditional approach) and concurrent evidence ('hot-tubbing'), the latter being covered by paragraph 11.1 of the Practice Direction to CPR35.

The Need
Going back to basics, the court's duty under CPR35.1 is to restrict expert evidence to that which is reasonably required to resolve the proceedings. The decision as to whether to permit oral evidence is normally taken at the listing stage, because, by that point, any challenge to an expert by way of CPR35 questions will be complete, and any application by the defendant to obtain evidence to put up against the claimant's expert will have been determined, with a joint report being prepared. Assuming that the experts have not reached a compromise position, the court might reasonably allow oral evidence for that issue to be determined between the parties, but that is not automatically the case. The issue might not have any bearing upon the ultimate determination of the claim. It might be disproportionate, or impracticable, for the experts to attend court to give their evidence. It might be that their opinions will depend on the judge's determination of material facts.

It goes without saying that the more money at stake (and, on a practical level, the time already allowed for trial of the case), the more likely the court will be to accommodate oral evidence, but that should never be taken as a given. The court will expect the parties to analyse the remaining issues between the experts and consider whether there is a compromise to be had. There is a danger that such a compromise will be sub-optimal and the parties will need to be alert to the possibility that, upon hearing evidence, the court will find new issues which fall to be determined and which require the input of the experts. Nevertheless, with the cost of experts often exceeding the cost of counsel attending court, there is a real interest in maintaining a sense of proportionality and seeing whether the experts actually need to attend.

When, in those circumstances, should they attend? As a rule, defendants fight cases for one of three reasons: (1) To discourage the next claim; (2) Irreconcilable differences; and (3) A failure to appreciate that the case does not fall into category (1) and/or (2). Whilst there is a suggestion of a fourth category where the respective solicitors hate each other, that is actually a combination of the three set out above: The animosity between the lawyers means that they want to win this case to discourage their opponent in the next claim, their positions become intractable and then irreconcilable, and as a result, they fail to appreciate that the particular case does not fall into either category. The same analysis applies to the calling of experts.

In some circumstances, the real issue is not the litigation before the court, but rather the emergence of a pattern of litigation. Sometimes, that is because the expert himself has acquired a dubious reputation for supporting a particularly challenging position. They hold an outlying opinion on a particular point of medicine, support claims which are inherently dubious, produce standard reports rather than bespoke reports, overstate the effects of the accident, or have simply tied themselves in knots both in their report and their CPR35 answers to the point where they need to be cross-examined. A single joint expert might well fall into this category if he has fallen into the trap of becoming an advocate for one side or the other. The cross-examining party is not simply trying to win this claim: they are trying to put down a marker on this action which they can rely upon in the next. A transcript of the expert's evidence will be obtained, as will a copy of the judgment if it is critical.

Of course, if the expert has written his report in accordance with CPR35, he should have nothing to worry about. By explaining why he rejects the contrary view (assuming that he can justify his position) he is unlikely to face the same degree of challenge. Courts are unlikely to permit cross-examination of an expert simply as a fishing trip to see how he might respond in the next case.

Also falling within category (1) are the cases where two renowned experts, habitually before the courts on opposite sides of the same point, join battle for yet another skirmish in their ongoing war of attrition. The point of principle falls to be determined by the court on the facts of the specific case, with the winner hoping that such a victory will lead to his opponent making concessions in other ongoing cases, not currently before the court. Does this cause have this effect? Is that effect *de minimis*? In effect, the parties are setting up a test case.

The second set of circumstances is where there is a real difference in opinion as to the effects of the accident, or the likely future prognosis, with a concomitant effect on the quantum of the claim. Those positions, of course, are likely to become more entrenched once suitable CPR36 offers have been made and the defendant is effectively pinning its hopes on its expert being preferred. It is, however, relatively obvious that the closer the parties are, the more likely that a commercial view of the case will be taken to resolve the matter without the experts needing to attend.

The discussion above tends to come about where the evidence goes to the question of quantum, but, of course, there may be reasons why an expert is required to determine the question of liability. In those circumstances, engineers might be required to attend court to explain why their methodology is preferable to that suggested by their opponent, or, particularly in the field of clinical negligence work, medical evidence might be required to determine whether the defendant fell within a reasonable body of medical opinion. It goes without saying that the court is far more likely to permit oral evidence from the experts in those circumstances.

In one recent case in my own practice, the claimant and each of the defendants had their own engineer, each opining on how the first defendant's employee had managed to lower the mast of a forklift truck on to the claimant, an employee of the second defendant, who had asked the first defendant's employee for assistance. The parties were well aware that the real questions were likely to be factual (re training, instructions given, the position of the claimant and the like) or legal (there being obvious contributory negligence, but subject to a judicial assessment as to the extent thereof) but the work equipment was far from standard (hence the accident) and the mechanics of the accident were such that some oral explanation was going to be required. The court, at the Pre-Trial Review, took the view that at least one expert had to be there to explain those nuances, and once that was the case, all three would need to be there, both in the interests of fairness and in order to give their views as to the respective control that the various individuals had over the situation. In fact, one defendant settled before the start of the trial, so that expert went home, leaving the other two to listen to the claimant's evidence, at which point the other defendant also settled the claim – no expert actually getting into the box.

Should one make an application?

In the normal course of events, the parties are aware of the potential need for the experts to attend court as far back as the case management conference at the beginning of the litigation, but the courts rarely give permission at that stage. The preference tends to be to determine the question at a Pre-Trial Review or, more realistically, on the filing of listing questionnaires. The parties are normally in agreement as to whether the experts will need to be called, and the court will normally be slow to interfere with that decision-making process. After all, the court has permitted each side to have an expert in the hope, rather than the expectation, that a joint report will produce a joint opinion. If the parties nevertheless wish their experts to attend court, they will need to be in a position to explain themselves when it comes to costs.

One obvious downside of the current trend in increasing court fees is that the cost of making a separate application to permit oral evidence is so significant that even if one side feels that oral evidence is unnecessary, they are more likely to consent than run the risk of an adverse costs order. Whilst the party wanting to call his expert is going to have to be in a position to explain to the court why that might be, the party who dismisses the idea will need to have good reason too – simply arguing proportionality is going to be of limited value if the evidence is supposedly central to the case.

The court may well insist that an application is made at the same time as the listing questionnaire. There is little to be done in such circumstances – the court has made that order and the fee will fall to be paid. If the application is contentious, then the parties will need to marshal their thoughts about the issues in the case and see whether the experts really are required.

GIVING EVIDENCE – THE TRADITIONAL APPROACH

As a matter of practicality, the court will need to hear all of the lay evidence in the case before hearing the expert evidence which arises from it. To insist that the claimant call his expert before hearing the defendant's version of events is so fraught with danger that there can only be very limited (and probably obvious) circumstances where it would be appropriate.

The question is then one of whether the experts should give evidence one after another, or whether they should give their evidence concurrently. It is worth setting out the traditional approach at this stage.

In the normal course of events, the claimant would call his expert first. The expert takes the oath, confirms his identity, qualifications and the truth of the opinions held in his reports. Whether or not he is allowed to expand on that evidence in chief is a matter for the court on the facts of the case, and he will be cross-examined by the defendant in an attempt to undermine his opinions and set up the defendant's case, to be delivered by its expert in due course. Re-examination might allow the claimant to deal with the specific issues to be relied upon by the defendant's expert if the court has not already given permission for the expert to expand on why he says that the defendant's expert is wrong in his evidence in chief. The procedure is then repeated for the defendant's expert.

The problems with the traditional approach are many and varied. The first is that there is, *prima facie*, an inequality of arms between the two sides – the second expert has the opportunity to assess which points have gone down well with the judge and thus need dealing with, and which points have failed to impress. He can tailor the tenor of his evidence, knowing when he can be reasonable and make concessions, and when he needs to be harder in his approach. The first expert is not afforded that luxury. On the other hand, if the first expert is hugely impressive, the second expert may have his work cut out to impress the court. In either event, there is the possibility that the damage to one side's case might lead to compromise without knowing how the second expert might fare.

The second problem is one of controlling the issues on which evidence is to be given. One might find that the first expert has to deal with a specific point in massive detail, only for it to become clear that there is actually nothing between the experts on that point and the real battleground is elsewhere. Much as one might like to think that the lawyers and the experts will have a full understanding of the subtleties of the case, there are often twists and turns to be had.

The third point is that very often an apparent difference between the experts is, in reality, a matter of linguistics or otherwise nuanced. To have the experts giving their evidence consecutively can make it difficult to ensure that the same issues are dealt with in the same way by both. Counsel cross-examining the expert is often being fed lines of attack by his own expert. That can lead to problems, because the expert, with respect to him, is unlikely to be an expert in how to cross-examine, and may not understand all of the wider issues in the case. On the other hand, counsel can find himself nothing more than cipher, potentially allowing experts with personal differences to settle scores by proxy.

HOT-TUBBING

In answer to those difficulties, and with the advent of active case management, the courts started to experiment with experts giving evidence concurrently. Over time, certain practices developed and 35PD.11 now sets out the appropriate procedure to be followed, although, of course, the court may take a more pro-active approach.

It is worth setting out the suggested methodology at this stage.

Firstly, the court may direct that the parties agree an agenda for the taking of concurrent evidence, based on the areas of disagreement identified in the joint statement made pursuant to CPR35.12.[1] Obviously, there may only be one area of disagreement between the experts, but even then there are potentially different arguments which each has used to reach his conclusion. The advantage of an agenda is clear – the parties can get to the nub of the issues between them and shorten the evidence by imposing a structure on the experts. Moreover, the fact that there is an agenda does not mean that it is finite – if some new point comes up, there is always a degree of flexibility to be had. The main benefit, however, is that the experts' respective views on the specific point can be canvassed at the same time, there can be cut and thrust between them if necessary, and there can be a measure of agreement reached.

Having agreed the agenda, the experts each take the oath or affirm, and they then address the items on the agenda as set out in paragraph 11.4 which provides that (subject to the judge's discretion to modify the procedure):

(1) The judge may initiate the discussion by asking the experts, in turn, for their views. Once the view is expressed, the judge may ask questions about it, bringing in the other expert as appropriate;

(2) After the judge has gone through that process for all the experts, the parties' representatives may ask questions of them, either testing the correctness of a view or clarifying it, but not covering ground already fully explored. The Practice Direction specifically notes that full cross-examination or re-examination is neither necessary nor appropriate;

---

1   Paragraph 11.2

(3) After that process, the judge may summarise the experts' different positions on the issue and ask them to confirm or correct that summary.

The obvious modification to that procedure might be that it be followed in respect of each point on the agenda in turn, rather than, as the PD appears to envisage, the entire agenda be covered by the judge and then by the advocates.

The other practical question to be addressed might be the running order of counsel in terms of cross-examination. A degree of flexibility is sensible here. It may be that the same running order is appropriate for each separate point. On the other hand, the party seeking to establish the specific point might seek to go first on the issue. On more than one occasion, instructed by a tortfeasor (D1) whose insurer (D2) had disavowed him, the situation has arisen where, with both claimant and second defendant having instructed engineers, the first defendant has had the first opportunity to challenge the experts, effectively being allowed to challenge both experts as necessary without being restricted by the obligation not to lead answers from one's own witness.

In practice, the success of hot-tubbing depends on a number of issues.

The first is that the judge has to be happy with the idea. That means that some time might need to be set aside for the court to come to terms with the specific issues to be covered. That, of course, can be dealt with most efficiently if the agenda can be drawn in advance and provided to the court for consideration in good time. The onus is therefore on the parties' representatives to address the issue in good time if practicable. If the joint report has been prepared properly, that should not be too difficult, although the lawyers should not be tempted to abdicate all responsibility to the experts on the point.

If there is to be a Pre-Trial Review (which would normally be before the trial judge), that would seem to be most sensible time to address the question of hot-tubbing. If the court is enthusiastic about the prospect, there will be some little time between the PTR and the trial in which agendas can be drawn and the experts prepared.

The second key to successful hot-tubbing is that the experts need to be open-minded about the process. The procedure is ideal if there is a large measure of agreement and they are, in fact, simply setting out the nuanced views at the end point of the argument. If, on the other hand, the experts are miles apart on the joint statement, the only hope is that by dint of being forced to sit side by side in the box, they will be able to rein in their worst excesses and reach the middle ground. Indeed, faced with two experts, one of whom is trying to be reasonable and one who is steadfast in his views, the court may well take the view that the latter is one whose agenda is not in accordance with the primary duty to the court.

The third key issue is the involvement of counsel. Hot-tubbing is still a relatively rare phenomenon and many lawyers are uncomfortable with the idea. Will my expert stand his ground? Are we going to appear weak? How can I control the narrative? These are all reasonable questions, but the answer lies in preparation. One can make sure that the agenda covers the relevant issues, and make sure that one understands both sides of the argument on any given point before the experts get in the box. The nub of it is, as suggested in the chapter on Joint Reports, that the expert needs to be in a position not only to expand on his own opinion, but also to enter into a legitimate critique of the opposing view. If he accepts it as a possibility, why does he prefer his own position? If he considers it beyond the pale, what's his basis for so doing? Knowing that one's expert understands the issue and can deal with it is key to the success of the hot-tubbing. If your view of the expert is that he won't stand up to that sort of debate, is this really a case which you want to take to trial?

It is important to realise that a case where both sides have experts attending trial is likely to be in multi track and is likely to have been the subject of cost budgeting. It is entirely proper to budget for pre-trial conferences with experts, but also, in preparation of the trial, drafting of the agenda.

There are two obvious complications to the basic 1 v 1 hot-tub scenario. The first is that there are more than 2 experts in that particular discipline. There is no reason why 3 or more experts should not undertake such an exercise. Indeed, the more experts, the more important it is that the court keep control over their evidence. One can foresee that on some points, two experts will form a (potentially short-lived) alliance against the third, only to retreat to their respective positions on the next issue. Overall, with a sensible agenda and reasonable judicial control being exercised, the overall effect should be to shorten the overall time for the giving of expert evidence.

The second complication arises where the experts are not, in fact, of the same discipline. That might be because the two sides have chosen to instruct experts from slightly different specialities. In some parts of the country, spinal surgery is performed by orthopaedic surgeons, whilst in others, neurosurgeons undertake the same operations. In some cases, one side might instruct a psychiatrist whilst the other might elect to instruct a psychologist. Those scenarios are relatively commonplace, but one might see the two sides going down radically different paths, one such case being where the claimant instructed an accountant to comment on his likely level of earnings as a professional boxer, whilst the defendant instructed an employment consultant who considered the statistical probabilities of success to be the primary issue, with the potential earnings at each level then falling into place. The case having settled before joint reports, one is left to speculate as to how they might have performed in the hot-tub.

Having observed hot-tubbing in action with both engineers and medical experts, one is driven to the conclusion that it is an entirely positive, but labour intensive, process which serves the best interests of justice. Whether it can be said to serve the best interest of the client depends, of course, on the result.

PART THREE

SPECIFIC
TYPES OF
EXPERT
EVIDENCE

Whilst each area of expertise potentially has a 'Trade Body', that does not mean that there is a consistency of approach to the provision of expert evidence. In order to acquire the necessary expertise, one often has to hold (or have held) a day job, whether as a surgeon, an engineer, an occupational therapist or the like, and those professional roles, whilst they might influence one's knowledge and approach to the problems that arise, do not train one to become an expert. For most experts, their involvement in litigation comes about because they have made a conscious decision to put themselves into that arena and have undergone some sort of formal training from outside their own trade to allow themselves to hold out as experts.

The formal requirements of providing an expert opinion are relatively straight-forward, as we have seen, but the practicalities of giving good expert evidence are much harder to learn. There are still experts who were giving evidence before the advent of the Civil Procedure Rules who went to court on a regular basis and honed their skills in that environment. There are experts who find themselves giving evidence in particularly difficult cases where, because of the money involved, both sides are habitually permitted evidence. They see other expert's reports on a regular basis and will form, even on a subconscious level, a view of what works and what does not.

For many experts, however, they are operating in a vacuum. Their early reports may be based on a precedent form obtained from a colleague, or provided by the solicitor or the people providing training, but they then have to take ownership of that format and make it work for them. A pull-down or delete-as-applicable template might work in the short-term, particularly if one is preparing relatively standard reports, but as soon as a degree of genuine expertise is required, a bespoke report is a necessity. One cannot opine on a spinal cord injury using tick boxes.

With that in mind, the final section of this book examines some of those areas where experts are commonly asked to report, in the hope that it provides guidance, or at least food for thought, so as to improve the quality and thus usefulness of expert reports. The opinions expressed are, of course, nothing more than that.

CHAPTER FIFTEEN
MOTOR ASSESSORS'
REPORTS

Nearly every road traffic accident will give rise to some sort of motor assessor's report. A claimant will want to get evidence about the value of his vehicle, the likely cost of repairs (and the cost-effectiveness of the same), whether temporary repairs are practicable and, if appropriate, the salvage value in the event that the vehicle is written off. Such reports are also obtained by the insurers, either in respect of their own insured vehicle or the claimant's vehicle. Twenty years ago, one might get a couple of photographs of the vehicle, taken with a cheap disposable camera. With the advent of digital cameras and high quality mobile phone imaging, such a report might also include a dozen or more photographs. The assessor has a dual role. He is, in the first instance, a witness of fact, recording the damage to a vehicle with due accuracy. His secondary role involves providing valuation evidence. Whilst that should be factual, there is an element of opinion to that assessment and I discuss that below.

The plethora of pictorial evidence, and a shift in insurers' perceptions, has given rise to a second type of motor assessor's report – the forensic engineer's report. That 'expert' is normally either an engineer or an assessor, although I have seen a metallurgist opine on such matters. In any event, their role is to consider the damage to one or both vehicles and to draw conclusions from that damage. I refer to them as engineers, as opposed to assessors.

Engineers might be looking to see whether all of the damage on a vehicle has been caused in one accident. They might be looking to see whether the damage to the two vehicles is consistent (or inconsistent) with them having hit each other. In multi-vehicle accidents, they might be asked to determine the order in which the impacts occurred. They might be asked to consider whether the damage is consistent with the occupants having suffered the personal injuries of which they complain (the Low Velocity Impact genre).

The main problem with such evidence is that the engineer is rarely afforded the optimal inspection conditions on which to found his opinion. In an ideal world, the engineer will inspect both vehicles, in person, at the same time. He will line them up, and take photographs of the two vehicles in their relative positions at impact. There will still, of course, be pitfalls. Was the road on an angle? How big were the occupants of the vehicles? What speed were the vehicles travelling at? Were they under braking? Was there any pre-existing damage or other compromise to their integrity? Nevertheless, such a report can have considerable import and effect.

In the real world, however, a vehicle might be scrapped, repaired, sold or otherwise 'disappeared' before that inspection can take place. The engineer might only have one vehicle from which to reach his conclusions. Normally, he will have to rely upon the photographs taken by the Assessor of one or both vehicles. Those photographs will have been stored digitally, but whether they can be provided in jpeg form (which can be manipulated to magnify the details) or pdf form (where magnification simply blurs the photograph) is another matter. The engineer is reliant upon the Assessor taking the right photographs, from the correct angles, and he cannot necessarily see the three dimensional aspects of the damage.

It is not normally the engineer's fault that the evidence is sub-optimal. An assessor's report is a cheap exercise, costing £50 to £100, whilst an engineer is likely to cost several times that, because his report is seen as an expert report and is therefore a bespoke product, rather than a pro forma, generic document. It follows that an engineer's report is normally only obtained when either the assessor, or somebody reading the assessor's report, considers that there might be something worthy of further enquiry – normally an inconsistency which might interest the insurer who might be liable to pay damages in respect of the accident. Unless the engineer is instructed quickly, the primary evidence can be lost.

Because the engineer's involvement normally stems from a suspicion that the original assessor's report shows an abnormality, the first engineer to be instructed is normally that chosen by the defendant/insurer. A whole host of issues arise, but the main one is that such a report runs a very real risk of being partisan. The insurer is likely to use engineers that it trusts to identify inconsistencies (because they are unlikely to instruct those who see no problems at all), and they do so in circumstances where they already have a *prima facie* suspicion about the *bona fides* of the claim. Once that suspicion is aroused, the engineer will inevitably have to engage in the intellectual challenge of looking afresh at evidence which he knows has only been made available to him because (a) the insurer is suspicious; (b) the insurer has chosen him to confirm its suspicions; and (c) the insurer habitually uses his services. Against that background, it is not hard to see how one's thought processes might be railroaded towards specific conclusions rather than identifying the forensic flaws in the examination process.

Thereafter, the claimant normally has to engage his own engineer in response. He, of course, suffers equal, but opposite, pressures. He might well identify problems with the data available, or inconsistencies in his opponent's assessments or conclusions. He might be doing that because he feels compelled to provide a fully balanced opinion to the court, but he might also feel compelled to obfuscate because there is no direct evidence of a negative to put up against a positive (but potentially poorly supported) conclusion.

A particular difficulty which befalls engineers is that, whilst one might be able to examine damage on a microscopic level, and the damage is static and therefore potentially there to see, each piece of metal will potentially react differently to any given circumstance. There is, inevitably, a plethora of alternatives and uncertainties, all flowing from a piece of evidence, normally a photograph, which appears, on its face, to be determinative.

Importantly, the engineer has to decide what he can actually see in the photographs, and in doing so introduces his own opinion, often at a stage before he realises that he is doing so. In one recent case, the assessor produced a series of photographs and concluded that the impact was at a slight angle rather than head on. The engineer, working solely from the photographs, concluded that the impact was head on and ignored the assessor's opinion. More worryingly, he also identified red paint transfer on various parts of the (black) vehicle. That red paint transfer formed a critical part of his opinion that the vehicle could not have been involved in an accident with a silver vehicle as alleged. No mention of red paint transfer was made on the assessor's report, predominantly because the red marks on the photographs were, in fact, reflections of the red rear lights of another vehicle, parked adjacent to the subject of the inspection. Whether that was the assessor's own vehicle was never made clear, but the deficits of a desk top assessment were obvious.

There are ways to avoid these problems. The most obvious one is for the engineers to be instructed at the same time, attend the vehicles together, discuss the damage and their potential conclusions and ensure that any *lacunae* in the evidence are addressed at an early stage. That is potentially a costly exercise, requiring some logistical effort, and it potentially nullifies the advantage of the first engineer inspecting the vehicles whilst the second has to use photographs. On the plus side, the court will then be presented with the best evidence in the case. Whether the parties are interested in presenting the best evidence is another matter.

The second method (equally obvious, and equally uncommon) would be for the reporting engineers to produce reports which actually set out the range of opinion rather than the end point of their argument. That means identifying the potential problems with the fact finding exercise. If the car is wet at the time that the photographs are taken, is that going to obscure the potential damage? If there are lights (red or otherwise) reflecting off the car, does that obscure the damage or confuse the viewer? If a bumper has been previously replaced, and might have been resprayed, might that explain the lack of lustre in the paintwork, or the fact that panels don't line up, or old paint colours showing through where the impact has caused the new paint to come away? What is direct damage and what is induced damage? Why might damage have been caused? If one identifies the range of opinion on such points, and then reaches a conclusion within that range, it is not a sign of weakness, but of reasoned analysis. It is, perhaps, unfortunate that those asked to provide reports on objective and observable evidence feel unable to accept that the range of opinion may still be nuanced.

Low Velocity Impact

I should make a confession here. Back in the late 1990's, I was sitting in the Blackpool County Court, watching plaintiff after plaintiff (as they were back then) step into the witness box and give very similar evidence as to how they had been affected by their whiplash injuries. I turned to my insurer client (who attended court with me on a regular basis) and muttered: "I wonder if you could get an engineer to prove that they couldn't have been injured?" Twelve months or so later, I saw my first LVI engineer's report. If the whole thing was my fault, I'm very sorry.

In any event, over the last 15 years or so, the insurance industry has committed significant resources to trying to prove that certain claimants were not, in fact, injured in their relatively modest road traffic accident, because they could not have been injured. Originally, there was an attempt to show that they could not have been injured *to the extent claimed*, but such nuances were almost impossible to prove, and the question became a more absolute one: "Could the claimant have been injured *at all* in this accident?"

Engineers instructed by defendants would seek to draw conclusions from the damage reported to the vehicles as to the likely speed at impact and thus the change in velocity (δv) in the target vehicle. From this, they opined as to the likely forces to be transferred to the claimant and whether those would suffice to cause injury.

There are, of course, a number of issues in such a case. Can the photographs, or the damage visible on inspection, give a definitive answer as to the relative speed of the vehicles, particularly as there might be a mass differential or a structural difference between the two bodies?

What if the claimant were not sitting in the optimal position? What if the impact had a lateral aspect giving a twisting effect? Older cars are constructed differently from newer models, and there is a potential issue as to the extent to which the impact is elastic, because in some low speed impacts (so the argument goes), the bumpers reform, maximising the transfer of kinetic energy, whilst at higher speeds the kinetic energy is dispersed because the vehicles disintegrate.

All of these factors cause potential uncertainty. It is, perhaps, no surprise that the Court of Appeal, in the case of *Armstrong et al v First York* [2005] EWCA Civ 277, held that it was for the trial judge to weigh such evidence in the balance when deciding the credibility of the claimants, but that he was not prohibited from accepting their evidence just because the (defendant's) expert said they could not have been injured.

It follows that, once again, the key to a successful report is to consider the range of opinion and discounting the impossibles, and then the improbables, before alighting on a conclusion, which is, as a result, far more fully argued and thus compelling. Of course, this may be reduced to historical significance only as the insurance industry lobbying might persuade the government to ban damages for whiplash completely, a legally and ethically challenging suggestion which goes beyond the scope of this book.

Format and Contents
The basic structure of an assessor's report is fairly standardised, albeit that a significant proportion of reports fail in one or more regards.

1. The maker of the report should identify himself and set out his qualifications, either at the start of the report or by way of an appendix. An astonishing percentage of assessors' reports fail even to identify the writer.

2. The writer should identify the vehicle which is the subject of the report and should provide appropriate data in terms of its mileage,

its general appearance, any pre-existing damage and the damage which is said to have been caused by the accident. A large number of reports ignore existing damage, which can only ever serve to mislead the reader and impact on the writer's *bona fides*. There is no reason why the report should not include several colour images showing not only the new damage but also the pre-existing condition of the car.

3. The writer should set out the damage which has been identified and the likely cost of repair, together with the salvage value if the vehicle is to be written off. He should identify the source of those figures, and in particular whether he has discussed the salvage value with the storing garage. Often that garage will have given consideration as to whether it might take the vehicle and repair it for their own ends. The claimant might be happy to get that salvage figure, but he might equally want to know the true value of his damaged vehicle and whether it might be repaired.

4. There should still be a Statement of Truth on the report. For the most part, the report is a factual one, but the calculation of value, repair costs and whether the vehicle should be written off is one of opinion and there is no reason why a report should not include a Statement of Truth.

The Range of Opinion

There are various issues where the reasonable assessor or engineer might proffer a range of opinion:

1. The first issue is as to the strength of the evidence available. If the inspection is hindered because of bad lighting, or the vehicle being parked in a difficult to access location, that should be set out, and attempts made to remedy it. If there's potential underlying damage, that can be the subject of comment.

2. The second is as to the means by which the car falls to be valued. There are a number of guides available, and there is a range of opinion as to whether one is looking at selling the car on the open

market, or to a dealer, or whether one is buying a car from a dealer. There is clearly an issue if a particular vehicle might only attract a modest offer from a dealer, who would then sell it at a premium. If a claimant has a 5 year old Ford Focus of a particular specification, should not his measure of loss be the cost of replacement? This is not a book about the measure of damages, but an assessor should surely offer some guidance as to the way in which the vehicle might be valued, rather than simply recording a figure which might have been plucked from thin air.

3. The third is as to the repair costs. These normally include a labour charge at a standard (or agreed) hourly rate. There is no reason why that should not be set out. It will include replacement parts. In the event of the vehicle being relatively new, it is inevitable that new parts will be required, but if the vehicle is an old one, there is no reason why consideration should not be given to using second hand parts. In some, rare, cases, that might be the only source of parts. To ignore the possibility that a second hand headlamp might only cost a fraction of the new unit, when the car itself is of modest value and thus stands to be written off is not to identify the range of opinion as to the cost of repairs. Similarly, if a panel can be repaired rather than replaced, the writer should consider that option. That is not to say that that is the only answer that should be put forward, but on an old vehicle which is a borderline constructive loss, there is no reason why an assessor cannot say: "To replace all damaged parts with new will cost £x and render this vehicle a constructive loss, but if one could source appropriate second hand parts, that will reduce to £y which would allow the vehicle to be repaired." There are arguments on both sides here: Should a claimant be entitled to replace old parts with new or be obliged to use second hand parts?

4. The fourth issue is as to what the claimant actually wants. Does the claimant actually want his vehicle written off? He might have owned the vehicle since new, and whilst its book value might be modest, he might know that he won't get an equivalent vehicle on the open market for the figure being suggested, so he might as well repair in any event. Is a claimant content to repair a panel rather

than replace it if it saves him £200? Assessors often work in a vacuum vis-à-vis the vehicle owner, because the vehicle is in a storage yard, and they often take the easy way out and give the maximum repair costs. That can lead to other issues: Is this car actually a write off, or is it just an attempt to force interim payment? A small variance in the initial valuation, the cost of repair and the salvage value can change a car from a repairable proposition to a write off. There is real potential for a conflict of interest between the storing garage (who might have a vested interest in keeping the client in a hire vehicle, or who might see the 'write off' as a repairable proposition to add to their fleet), the insurer (who, on a fully comprehensive policy, might want to keep its own liability down) and the client, who may well find himself cut out of the loop.

5. The fifth issue is as to whether there is scope for a temporary repair. The assessor might not consider that a temporary repair is feasible, but what about a partial repair? There might be an additional cost involved in doing something twice, but if a modest payment might suffice to render the car roadworthy, even if that is not the most cost-effective, should it not be considered if the wider picture is a significant ongoing hire claim?

6. In terms of consistency of damage, engineers should be careful to set out the various possibilities, whether as to what the damage might be, or how the damage might have been caused, or whether that is compatible with the damage to the other vehicle. It is easy, for instance, to look at two badly damaged cars where the damage profile on the two vehicles is both a different shape and at different heights and opine that the damage is inconsistent because no part of vehicle A could have come into contact with vehicle B, but that is not the same as an engineer concluding that the vehicles could have come together but not causing this damage. It is imperative to set out what is possible and what is impossible before offering an opinion as to what, on balance, has happened. If one is unnecessarily definitive in the original opinion, there is always the risk that other possibilities will be canvassed in cross-examination, leaving the expert having to justify his robust opinions and those he excluded.

In one recent case, the expert alighted on the phrase 'Not necessarily' in response to alternatives being put. "This could have happened?" "Not necessarily." "Well is it possible?" "Not necessarily." "Well if it's not necessarily possible, are you saying that it's impossible?" "Not necessarily." "So it's possible then?" "Not necessarily."

7. In cases where LVI might be an issue, the crux will be the extent to which the deformation and reformation of parts is consistent with certain impact speeds and the concomitant elasticity of the collision. That, in turn, might allow an expert to opine as to the plausible range of δv in the case. The sensible expert would be well advised to compare those forces to day to day activities which people undertake, although it would be naïve to suggest that those day to day activities are incapable of causing injury – one can put one's back out sneezing if that leads to an unexpected movement. Ultimately, engineers can probably only go so far with their opinions in such cases, before the matter becomes one for the medical experts, or the judge.

    Ultimately, the engineer who sets out the range of opinion and then explains why he rejects the alternatives and thus alights on his conclusion is likely to come across as more reasonable and more convincing than the engineer who alights on his conclusion and rejects all alternatives, only then to have to justify why. The expert who tells the court that only he can be right runs the risk of challenging the Judge to find him wrong.

CHAPTER SIXTEEN
ACCIDENT RECONSTRUCTION
REPORTS

Whilst the motor assessor's report is almost ubiquitous in road traffic litigation, a report reconstructing events is a far rarer beast. The reasons are twofold: On the one hand, there is a significant cost involved in providing such a report, particularly as regards the gathering and consideration of evidence, and, on the other, there is the obvious fact that the courts would much prefer to decide cases on the evidence of the witnesses who were there and can give their impression of events, no matter how imperfect that might be.

The latter point was reinforced in the case of *Liddell v Middleton*[1] where Stuart-Smith LJ gave what has become the definitive analysis of the role of an engineer in such a case:

"In such cases the function of the expert is to furnish the judge with the necessary scientific criteria and assistance based upon his special skill and experience not possessed by ordinary laymen to enable the judge to interpret the factual evidence of the marks on the road, the damage or whatever it may be. What he is not entitled to do is to say in effect, 'I have considered the statements and special evidence of the eyewitnesses in this case and I conclude from their evidence that the defendant was going at a certain speed, or that he could have seen the plaintiff at a certain point.' These are facts for the trial judge to find based on the evidence that he accepts and such inferences as he draws from the primary facts found. Still less is the expert entitled to say that in his opinion the defendant should have sounded his horn, seen the plaintiff before he did or taken avoiding action and that in taking some action or failing to take some other action, a party was guilty of negligence. These are matters for the court, on which the expert's opinion is wholly irrelevant and therefore inadmissible."

That paragraph has, of course, been used in respect of practically all types of expert evidence, but it is here, in this chapter, where it belongs.

1[1996] PIQR 36

The first thing to note is that reconstruction evidence is unlikely to be obtained in cases of modest value. The real use of such evidence tends to be in cases where the claimant, for whatever reason, cannot give direct evidence as to the circumstances of the accident. Obviously there are cases where one or more of the parties suffered fatal injuries in the accident, but clearly there are cases where a party might have no recollection, either as a result of a head injury or inebriation, and there are also cases where there is almost too much information, with conflicting factual versions from various witnesses, which are impossible to reconcile, save by relating same to the physical evidence which is available. If a claimant has suffered significant injuries, then proportionality arguments about the need for such evidence are unlikely to succeed, but the courts will nevertheless be careful to consider whether such evidence is actually required to allow a determination of liability in any given case.

It is worth mentioning how often lay witnesses actually give their opinions in such cases without being criticised for it. A lay assessment of time, distance or the speed of a vehicle, whether the observer is a pedestrian, a passenger or an oncoming driver, might have some qualitative (albeit subjective) accuracy but is unlikely to be objectively quantitative.

At one end of the spectrum, one has the witness given to hyperbole: "He came from nowhere – he was driving like a maniac!" had to be revisited when the counter came: "I was driving an electric truck. It has no speedometer because you don't need one if your top speed, unladen, is less than 8mph. I had a half ton trailer on the back." At the other, the witness who said, "At that point he was 28 feet back from the junction" was challenged as to how he could be so accurate. "I've been a quantity surveyor for 35 years;" came the reply, "it was 28 feet."

Whilst neither witness was giving evidence in a case involving reconstruction evidence, any expert would be reliant upon the judge's findings of fact before he could finalise his opinion if that information formed part of his assessment. In the normal course of events, the Judge reaches a conclusion without further information.

What is, perhaps, interesting about the reconstruction report genre is that most such reports rely, at their heart, on relatively simple mathematical formulae to calculate distances travelled during specific periods of time (normally under putative braking) based on the physical evidence. Those equations are on the GCSE Physics syllabus and might reasonably be within the understanding of an ordinary layman or judge. Unlike a medical report where specific graduate level training might be required to understand the specific injuries involved, anybody playing with toy cars, or driving their own vehicle, will have some basic understanding of the issues in play, if only at a subconscious level.

The special knowledge of the expert is not, therefore, the mathematics themselves, but the assessment of the physical data which can then be fed into the equations. His experience will allow him to opine on the likely coefficient of friction on the road surface in specific conditions, or the effects of apparent defects in tyres. He can give his opinion as to the likely reaction times, although that is potentially more problematic: Such data is relatively freely available insofar as it relates to the general population, but the specific reactions of the driver will be personal and depend on relative trivialities which might be forgotten when trying to recall a traumatic event. The fraction of second spent glancing in the rear view mirror as part of the care and skill to be exercised by the reasonable and careful driver might be critical when it coincides with a pedestrian stepping out from behind a car. The expert may be able to comment on perspicuity, but only in cases where he brings additional knowledge and understanding to bear rather than simply opining on what one can or cannot see. That opinion is, in all likelihood, to be based on his interpretation of photographic evidence which is available to the court, and the court is unlikely to allow itself to be usurped in that way.

The reconstruction expert really comes into his own when the theoretical mathematics is complicated by the physical reality of a situation. The theoretical mathematician works with single points of mass, normally in a vacuum or in a frictionless environment. The mathematics is absolute. The real world does not work that way. A pedestrian's centre of mass is unlikely to be the first point to impact with an oncoming vehicle. The friction of a road surface might be compromised by the weather conditions. The deceleration of the car is not necessarily linear. The blow might be glancing, causing rotational movement as well as lateral. There may be other data available to an expert in the form of an on-board computer or the extent (or location) of impact damage which can only be assessed by somebody with appropriate expertise. The skill of the reconstruction expert is therefore to take information, to discern its meaning and thereafter to calculate those matters which will allow the court to reach its own conclusions – normally the far more simplistic speed, distance and time.

One difficulty that the expert often has in such cases is in expressing that opinion in an accessible manner. Taking height out of the equation (as most accidents occur at ground level), one still has to account for road position, distances travelled and, critically, the timing of events. To convey those remaining three dimensions in a two-dimensional paper report is potentially the most challenging aspect of the role of the reconstruction expert. Whilst a video presentation might explain the nuances, the reports are almost inevitably reduced to writing with the constraints that that involves. There are ways of expressing the data in two-dimensional form, but often one needs to have specific expertise and experience to understand the report.

That becomes particularly important because the critical moment in a sizeable proportion (if not the overwhelming majority) of road traffic accidents is not the point of impact, but some point (or more likely points) in the five seconds or so immediately before, when the die is cast. What made the driver decide to travel at that speed? What caused the driver to react? Where was the other party at that point? What else was going on *at that point*? The eye witness is rarely aware of the impending accident at that point in time and will be reliant on *ex post facto* reconstruction once aware that the accident has occurred. It is all too easy for the witness, the lawyers, the court and even the experts to focus on the dynamics of one vehicle (normally the alleged tortfeasor) whilst not paying full attention to the dynamic position of the other party. Whilst it potentially requires a number of diagrams (and thus time-consuming work on the part of the expert) to give the best explanation of the mechanics of an accident, one has to consider time as, perhaps, the critical dimension in any such case. The expert who can convey the chronology of events in the clearest manner will inevitably have the ear of the judge when it comes to expressing his opinion.

The main difficulty with reconstruction experts is deciding when they should attend trial. There is an inevitably considerable expense involved in them attending, particularly if they are, on paper agreed, but particular care has to be taken in that regard if there needs to be a determination of the lay evidence upon which they are to opine. They might be able to deal with that by offering views depending on various scenarios which might be open to the court to find, but there remains the risk that until the evidence is heard, the experts rely upon their own views of the evidence rather than the reality of the situation: A contemporaneous statement from a police driver stating that four pedestrians ran out diagonally towards him in a line from his left, such that whilst he swerved to avoid them he was unable to avoid the fourth individual, caused huge confusion because both experts (and the various lawyers on both sides) interpreted him as meaning that they had entered the carriageway in single file, such that if he missed the first three, there was no way in which he could hit the fourth. The experts having reached agreement on that basis, they did not attend trial, leaving the officer trying, in vain, to explain that he meant (albeit that he had never been asked to clarify) that they ran out in a phalanx, with the fourth furthest into the road. The experts had already opined that the driver must have been mistaken in his recollection because they had both (mis)understood the statement differently.

It follows that even in a case where the reconstruction evidence appears relatively clear and there is agreement between the experts, the lawyers should ensure that the reports set out a full range of opinion which may, by necessity, include a range of scenarios.

Format and Contents

The majority of reconstruction experts are well established, highly regarded individuals who garner instructions by the quality of their reports. Those reports tend to follow relatively standardised structures, notwithstanding the potential range of accidents which might be considered.

As a preliminary point, the purpose of the report should be identified, albeit in careful and neutral terms. There is a danger here that the wrong question is asked, but if the report writer can identified that error at the earliest possible stage, objectivity can be maintained. To give an example, if the purpose of the report is given as "*To consider the relative movements of vehicle 1 and vehicle 2 during the accident with a view to identifying their respective speeds and the potential sight lines of the two drivers in the period before the collision*" one can see that the question is neutrally phrased, whilst if the purpose is given as "*To consider the likely path of vehicle 2 and whether the driver of vehicle 1 should have seen his approach and avoided the collision*" there is an inherent bias in the question which can only lead to trouble.

Thereafter:
1. The evidence available to the expert should be identified. That evidence should, if possible, include:
    a. Contemporaneous photographs of the scene to include any specific damage or marks on the road;
    b. Contemporaneous photographs of the vehicles (if available);
    c. Any police report or interview notes;
    d. Any assessors' reports as to vehicle damage;
    e. The Statements of Case from the action (if available);
    f. The witness statements within the action (if available);
    g. The medical reports within the action insofar as they might set out:
        i. The history of the accident as reported by the claimant;
        ii. The physical injuries to the claimant which might go to evidence the mechanism of the accident. In most cases where reconstruction evidence is likely to

be required, it should be obvious to the claimant's solicitors at a relatively early stage and there is no reason why the examining experts should not be asked to pay particular attention to the nature of the injuries sustained insofar as they can, and the physical nature of the claimant both in terms of height (which might go to view) and weight/build (which might be part of the required equations).

2. The evidence which the expert himself has obtained should be identified. That evidence is likely to include:
    a. Maps and aerial photographs of the accident, giving an overview of the location;
    b. Photographs taken at regular distances leading up to the accident location from both directions, together with any other appropriate views, preferably taken from a representative position (i.e. if one is looking at a driver's view, from his likely position in the vehicle, or in the case of a pedestrian, from their approximately height). If the accident occurred at night, but the area is relatively well-lit, consideration should be given to obtaining photographs in similar circumstances to those prevailing at the relevant time, although that is potentially difficult, time-consuming and unhelpful. It may, of course, be the case that the police are able to provide such photographs in any event;
    c. Close up photographs of any relevant damage to the vehicles (if available).

    d. A consideration of the lay evidence, albeit that this will need to be approached with care (see above). The expert needs to appreciate that the evidence has not yet been tested, that there might be inaccuracies or anomalies within the evidence, and that the court might have to make a determination of the facts before proceeding to the next stage. The safest course may well be to use the lay evidence to set the scene of the accident in qualitative terms, but to acknowledge that when it comes to detail, as an expert one can only draw conclusions from the objective and certain evidence available.

3. The expert should thereafter be in a position to set out the conflicting positions of the parties if such is the case, and can legitimately set out the areas of factual dispute which fall to be determined by the judge. That uncertainty should be highlighted before moving on to the range of opinion.

4. Having set out the range of opinion (see below), in reaching (and expressing) conclusions the expert should bear in mind that those reading his conclusions will need to visualise the events if they are to understand them. Burying opinion within data, particularly in written form, makes it difficult to comprehend. There might be a good reason for an expert to express his views in convoluted form, but there is no reason why a genuinely held view cannot be expressed simply. Diagrams, and particularly a series of diagrams showing either progression over time or alternative scenarios, are a potentially compelling method to convey the analysis of the accident.

5. Critically, it is important to acknowledge that one party's vision and reaction time might be very different from that of the other. A younger driver might have quicker reactions – it does not make the older driver negligent. The driver trying to pick out a pedestrian in dark clothing on an unlit road will have a harder time seeing the pedestrian than the pedestrian will have trying to see the oncoming headlights. The overtaking motorcyclist with the car in front of him will have a better chance than the driver trying to identify what is happening behind him whilst concentrating on what is going on ahead of him. This potentially becomes even more important where a driver is having to use his mirrors. At which mirror must he be looking at any given point in time? For how long would the motorcyclist be in view in that mirror?

6. If there is some mathematical complexity to the analysis, there is no reason why that should not be set out in an appendix to the report if it keeps the report itself to a sensible length.

The Range of Opinion

There are various issues where the reasonable reconstruction expert might proffer a range of opinion:

1. The first issue is as to the strength of the evidence available. If the contemporaneous evidence is sub-optimal, or inconsistent, or the scene has changed since the accident, that should be the subject of comment. If the evidence is, for whatever reason, weak, such that the expert needs to acknowledge that by including variables in his equations or conclusions, there is no reason not to say so. If findings of fact need to be made by the court before the expert's opinion can bite, there is no reason not to set out those alternatives with the opinions which would follow in any given scenario.

2. The second issue is as to the consistency of the evidence available. It is not for the expert to start passing comment on internal inconsistencies in a party's evidence, but his role inevitably extends to consideration of the objective evidence as he sees it to see whether it tallies with the lay evidence. He should identify the potential inconsistency as a matter which falls to be determined by the court, but can legitimately opine, for instance, that the height of the impact damage on the front-pillar of the car is consistent with an impact speed of x mph rather than the witness's estimate of y mph which might reasonably have seen the pedestrian pass over the roof of the car.

3. The third issue is as to the timing of events. There will inevitably be a range of thinking times and speeds, and distances covered, because no expert could give an absolute answer without particularly cogent objective evidence. The range of opinion as to, say, thinking times, might mean that one has to set out calculations at either end of the spectrum before opining as to one's particular preference. That will inevitably have a knock on effect on the relative distances travelled by the parties before impact. As mentioned above, one should consider the possibility that one party will be able to react more quickly than the other. A flexible approach is required to allow for the court

to make the requisite findings once it has reached conclusions as to the basic facts.

4. The fourth area which experts should consider and identify the range of opinion is as to what a party might be able to see and how they might react to it. What triggered the driver's response? What might (or should) have triggered the driver's response? A driver might not recall seeing the hazard until impact, but if he has stopped impossibly quickly after impact, he must already have been reacting to something. This potentially falls under the question of consistency of evidence as set out at (2) above, but the question of why drivers react as they do is something which is reasonably within the purview of a reconstruction expert. He should be careful to analyse the various possibilities before alighting on his conclusions.

Ultimately, as ever, the expert who sets out the range of opinion and then explains why he rejects the alternatives and thus alights on his conclusion is likely to come across as more reasonable and more convincing than the expert who alights on his conclusion and rejects all alternatives, only then to have to justify why.

CHAPTER SEVENTEEN
ENGINEERING EVIDENCE
(EMPLOYERS' LIABILITY CLAIMS)

One of the most common types of personal injury claim is the injury sustained at work. Many of those cases turn on questions of fact, or an assessment of the law (or blameworthiness) by the judge, rather than requiring expert evidence from an engineer, and there is often a legitimate question as to the extent to which the engineer is giving an opinion as opposed to explaining the circumstances of the accident to the court. The maxim that "judges, not experts, decide cases" is often the best place to start when considering the role of an engineer in such a case.

In general terms, such claims fall into one or more of the following 6 categories:
1. Injury caused by the negligence of a fellow employee for whom the employer is vicariously liable;
2. Injury caused by the use of the premises (normally a trip or slip);
3. Injury caused by the state of the premises (again, normally a trip or slip);
4. Injury caused by interaction with work equipment;
5. Injury caused by working method (normally lifting claims);
6. Injury caused by exposure to a risk over time (disease claims).

In categories 1 and 2 (assuming that no other category is engaged), it is hard to see how an engineer might assist the court. Whether a box was left where somebody could fall over it is not a matter for expert opinion in the normal course of events.

The state of premises
In category 3 cases, the role of the expert is normally by way of commentary on the construction of the premises, either as to the surface or gradient of the floor. That commentary, however, is often constrained to taking measurements (e.g. the friction coefficient of the floor surface) and reporting on specialist facts, such as the requirements of British

Standards as applicable at any given point in time and the extent to which new standards might be retrospective. The requirement for opinion evidence in its purist form tends to be limited to questions of practicability: Is it possible to improve the friction of that surface? Is that an appropriate surface in the circumstances? Are other surfaces better or worse and why?

That is not to say that experts are unnecessary in such cases, but the court may well take the view that a single joint expert is the appropriate way in which to obtain that evidence.

Interaction with work equipment

Many accidents involve employees injuring themselves in the machines with which they work. The mechanism of such injuries is often far from clear, because the machine is normally designed not to pose an immediate risk to anybody who comes into contact with it. The role of the engineer in those circumstances is often to document the workings of the machine, identify how the accident occurred, identify why the accident might have occurred (which might include apparent failings on the part of either party), and what steps might reasonably have been taken to prevent the accident or reduce the risk of it happening. Labelled photographs or diagrams, explaining the terminology of the machinery in question is often of immense help to the court, which would otherwise have to struggle with rendering what can be seen and identified on a photograph into a text which might form the critical part of a judgment.

It is not, however, the role of the expert to opine as to the relative blameworthiness of the people involved. Stating that "It should have been obvious to the claimant that this was dangerous" is not normally an opinion which is necessarily within the engineer's remit. This can, on occasion, be avoided by the wording of the case management order, but in any event the writer of a report needs to appreciate that the question is very much one for the court.

Working method

This is an area where the expert might reasonably provide useful opinion evidence, again predicated upon his factual findings. Identifying the appropriate range of working methods and the capacity of individuals to cope with those methods should form the foundation of the report, with the specific facts as they apply to the claimant in question being set out. It is legitimate in those circumstances to proffer opinion as to whether the task in question fell within what was permissible or advised, but the expert should be careful to set out as much information in support of that opinion as he can.

Disease

The role of an expert in such a case has been discussed earlier in this work, when the question of the timing of a report was considered. There are various types of disease, including Work Related Upper Limb Disorders, Noise Induced Hearing Loss, Dermatitis and Mesothelioma. In each case, the role of the expert will include identifying the relevant standards, opining as to the situation in which the claimant found himself, the nature of his exposure to risk and/or the factual questions to be determined to identify the level of exposure, and his opinion as to whether or not there was an actionable level of exposure. In NIHL cases, the engineer should identify the likely level of noise, rather than simply ducking the issue and saying that he cannot say whether or not the levels were actionable. The question should be asked of him, at the time of his instruction (and/or on the face of the case management order): "Please give your opinion as to the claimant's likely exposure to noise during each employment and/or the facts which the court will need to determine to reach the necessary findings." All too often, thousands of pounds are spent, only for an engineer to say: "I can't say that he was exposed to excessive noise". The engineer should not simply abdicate responsibility in those circumstances.

Format and Contents

The role of an engineer in this sort of case is often that of the experimenting scientist, and the report can reasonably read as if it were the write-up of an experiment, without unnecessary commentary. One of the problems with such reports is that the expert can feel almost underused, because that which is required of him is actually fairly limited. Taking measurements and reporting on them rarely constitutes opinion, and it often difficult to resist the temptation to offer a view when, in reality, that is a matter for the court. The best reports keep things as simple as possible.

1. The purpose of the report should be identified: e.g. *In this case I am asked to measure the co-efficient of friction of the floor surface in the main entrance hall of the defendant's premises, having regard to the possible prevailing weather conditions and the footwear provided to the claimant for use at work. I am asked to opine as to whether the floor covering in use complied with the relevant British Standards, the practicability of altering or replacing that flooring with a safer alternative, and the potential effects of alternative flooring solutions given the facts of the current case.*

2. The evidence available to the expert should be identified. That evidence should, if possible, include:
   a. Any contemporaneous pictures or plans of the location or work equipment;
   b. Any relevant documentation pertaining to the selection, provision, installation and/or maintenance of the premises or work equipment;
   c. The Statements of Case from the action (if available);
   d. The witness statements within the action (if available);
   e. The medical reports within the action insofar as they might set out:
      i. The history of the accident as reported by the claimant;
      ii. The physical injuries to the claimant which might go to evidence the mechanism of the accident.

3. The statutory framework should be identified, setting out the chronological development (which is particularly appropriate in disease cases where exposure may straddle different statutory regimes) and the extent to which changes were retrospective.

4. The evidence which the expert himself has obtained should be identified. That evidence is likely to include:
    a. Photographs and plans of the location. These are often of limited value to the expert, but the parties and the court find them of assistance in setting the scene;
    b. The methods used by the expert in his investigation;
    c. The factual findings of the investigation.

5. A consideration of the lay evidence, and any conflicts therein, should be set out. As in the previous chapters, if the evidence has not been tested, it will need to be treated with care. Again, the safest course may well be to use the lay evidence to set the scene of the accident in qualitative terms, but to acknowledge that, when it comes to detail, as an expert one can only draw conclusions from the objective and certain evidence available. The expert can legitimately set out opinions based on the respective factual matrices, so that the court might identify the version that it prefers and proceed accordingly. In writing the report, the expert should consider himself a facilitator for the court, providing the necessary guidance and explanations, but acknowledging that in these circumstances, he is very much there to assist the court by providing insider knowledge as to the engineering aspects of the case. It may, of course, be that the judge has particular understanding and expertise in any event.

6. Having set out the range of opinion (see below), in reaching (and expressing) conclusions the expert should bear in mind that those reading his conclusions need to understand them. Burying opinion within data, particularly in written form, makes it difficult to comprehend. The need for a summary of the expert's conclusions is of particular import in such reports and, if the analysis within the body of the report is sufficiently detailed, there is no reason why the conclusion should not be distilled to the bare bones, stripping out unnecessary comment which can often stray beyond the expert's remit.

7. If there is some mathematical complexity to the analysis, there is no reason why that should not be set out in an Appendix to the report

if it keeps the report itself to a sensible length. Similarly, the photo-graphs (if appropriate) can be in an Appendix.

The Range of Opinion

Very often the range of opinion is actually rather limited in such cases, but that does not absolve the expert from addressing the question. The reality may be that the real variability pertains to the factual matrix, in which case the report should set out the further information which is required to give a more definitive opinion.

One thing which is rarely seen in such reports, but is of potential use, is an indication by the expert as to whether he would benefit from hearing oral evidence before reaching his conclusion or whether the questions to be answered are sufficiently binary to allow the court to make those determinations and then apply the results. Whilst that is not going to determine the question of whether the expert should attend trial, it both assists the court on that question and focuses the expert's mind on what he's actually being asked to do.

CHAPTER EIGHTEEN
CLINICAL NEGLIGENCE
(LIABILITY) REPORTS

Whilst the preponderance of reports from medical experts pertain to condition and prognosis, in cases where the claim arises from allegedly negligent clinical care expert evidence is required on the question of liability. These reports form the basis of the entire case, and there are extra layers of content and difficulty which attach. Those asked to report are normally senior experts in their field, not least because they are being asked to provide an opinion on their fellow professionals, and there is inevitably a risk that their undoubted experience leads them to a view as to the best course of action in any given circumstance. That is what makes them an expert in their field. It also creates a potential danger when it comes to producing a liability report, because, of course, the test in clinical negligence claims pertains to what a reasonable body of professional opinion would do,[1] as long as it was not illogical or unreasonable.[2] That means that the reporting expert is not there to identify the optimum methodology, but to consider, quite deliberately, sub-optimal, but acceptable, conduct within that field of expertise.

Clinical negligence claims, in broad terms, are either cases where procedures have gone wrong by reason of negligent acts, or claims where there have been omissions in the care, which have led to a failure to treat timeously, appropriately or at all. There are also claims which deal with the issue of consent, which potentially warrant a chapter of their own. For these purposes, they are, in effect, negligent omissions.

Negligent Acts
In the first class of cases, the necessary analysis boils down to whether or not a reasonably competent body of medical expertise would have committed that negligent act. The expert needs to comment on acceptable risk within a procedure and whether the event occurred irrespective of the acts of the doctor involved.

---

1   *Bolam v Friern Hospital Management Committee* [1957] 1 WLR 582

2   *Bolitho v City and Hackney Health Authority* [1996] 4 All ER 771

In this sort of case, the analysis really needs to start by explaining why the patient was undergoing the procedure, what the procedure involves (preferably in layman's terms as well as technical), and the range of likely outcomes (and the chances of any given outcome). It should then identify the acceptable risks (which often stem from the fact that the patient, if well, would not have been undergoing a procedure in the first place), and then identify what actually happened, before concluding whether or not that was outwith the reasonable range of medical expertise.

Instead, such reports often identify some sort of 'but for' test and then blame the doctor for not taking that step: "Had you sent the sample off to the lab on the Thursday night and marked it urgent, you could have informed the patient on Friday afternoon that she had this problem, ergo your failure to send the sample until the timetabled pickup on Friday lunchtime which meant that it was Monday before you got the results caused the problem" is not *prima facie* evidence of negligence.

Negligent Omissions

This is often a more difficult scenario, because the analysis is inevitably conducted in hindsight. When one knows that the outcome of events was negative, the natural response is to try to identify what went wrong and how that result might have been avoided. That is not, however, the test which the court needs to apply in such cases. What the court needs to understand is how a doctor, presented with that patient with that history, those complaints and those risks, might reasonably have acted at that point in time.

In such cases, the chronology is critical, and the simplest and most compelling reports are those which set out the developing situation and the range of reasonable opinion at any given point in time, whether by reference to Occam's Razor or otherwise. If the patient had a relatively common presentation, a reasonable body of doctors would consider it, in the first instance, to be that common complaint. Undertaking common tests and failing to spot that the patient actually has a rare condition is not necessarily negligent. Again, setting out the range of opinion pursuant to 35PD.2(6) is critical to a high quality report, in this case because by identifying what various doctors *might have* done in those circumstances, the reasonableness of what *was* done can be ascertained.

Form and Contents

1. As ever with reports which go to the question of liability, the purpose of the report needs to be identified. If a report of this nature correctly identifies what is to be considered and the potential purpose of the report, everything else should fall into place. *"In this case I am asked to consider whether the way in which the defendant treated the claimant and investigated his complaints from time to time fell within or outside the conduct of a reasonable body of medical opinion."*

2. The evidence available to the expert should be identified, with specific reference to the source of that evidence, particularly if the claimant has been treated at various different locations, and the dates covered by those records. In such cases, inevitably, the emphasis will be on the medical notes, because the claimant's history will be both subjective and given in hindsight. One could even argue that the claimant's history should not be considered in determining what actually happened, because, as evidence which forms part of the legal analysis, it is almost certainly flawed.

3. The report should then set out the chronology of events, having regard to the medical records and the information provided by the claimant. The source of information should be identified (because, as discussed, some information might be more objective), and the expert should comment at each stage (or at least at each critical stage) as to:
   (a) What has occurred and the situation in which the doctor found himself;
   (b) The range of actions which a reasonable doctor would consider at that specific point in time, with the potential outcomes from those actions;
   (c) The action actually taken by the doctor (identifying whether it was outwith the reasonable range of options);

(d) The effects of that action and the cumulative effects of the actions up to that point.

By being transparent in this way, the litigants and the court can see precisely where the critical failings occurred and their results. If the answer is that any given action might have been reasonable, but the totality of the actions was not, say so. If the answer is that the totality of the actions was sub-optimal, but within an acceptable range of opinion, say so.

The Range of Opinion

One might reasonably expect an expert in the field to be at the forefront of current medical understanding, but it is inevitable that new techniques and practices will develop and that established experts might prefer the methods which they know and trust. It is potentially very difficult to assess, with hindsight, the precise state of medical understanding at the time of events where science has advanced (and/or funding regressed) in the intervening period. It can be helpful for an expert to identify the current state of understanding as well as that at the time of the events complained of, because often the issue between the parties is as to whether current thinking should have been applied at an earlier point in time.

As ever, the more rational and detailed the analysis of the expert, and the more clearly that he sets out the range of opinion, the more compelling his evidence will be.

CHAPTER NINETEEN
MEDICAL REPORTS (GENERAL)

The assessment of damages for pain, suffering and loss of amenity is, in English law, a function of both diagnosis and prognosis. The main three issues in valuing an injury are (1) the nature of the injury and the level of any ongoing disability; (2) the recovery period if recovery is expected; and (3) the potential for long-term deterioration.

Practically every personal injury case will involve at least one medical report, the purpose of which, at least in theory, is fourfold:

1.   To confirm that the person making the claim is who they claim to be ("identification");

2.   To give a diagnosis of the injury of which the claimant complains ("diagnosis");

3.   To confirm that the injury of which the claimant complains was caused by the alleged tort ("causation"); and

4.   To give a prognosis for that injury to facilitate the assessment of damages payable ("prognosis").

This chapter concentrates on orthopaedic and soft tissue injuries, firstly because they are the most commonly seen, and secondly because the issues which they raise are relatively generic and can be applied to other fields with very little modification. The following chapter deals with the specific and interesting question of ENT reports in NIHL cases.

IDENTIFICATION

Whilst most experts probably give little thought to this issue on a day to day basis, this is actually fundamental to the provision of a medical report. If the claimant's claims are subjective, the veracity of the claimant is central, and whilst the objective reader might find it implausible, it is not unknown for claimants to make claims under aliases (to facilitate multiple claims being made, either concurrently or consecutively) or have others attend their medical appointments for them to ensure that their (well rehearsed) complaints are rehearsed well to the examiner.

I have seen a man give his first and fourth names as his "full name" and aver that he was living at address A, but then present a full set of medical notes using just his middle two names and placing him at address B. I have read the medical records and medical reports of a man whose height varied from 5'1" to 5'8" and back again over a 6 year period.[1] I have heard tales of a woman with a particularly unusual congenital deformity in her neck who presented herself for examination by the same expert on different occasions using different names. I have appeared in numerous cases where one party has denied that the person making the claim was the person present at the material time.

In each case, the identity and description of the person making the complaint assumes real import. The basics are relatively straight-forward. One might reasonably expect to see the name, address, date of birth[2] and gender of the claimant on the front of the report. Height, weight, build, dominant hand (particularly in upper limb injuries) and distinguishing features are not unreasonable identifiers, particularly in reports involving physical examination.[3] A record of their appearance and demeanour is potentially part of the assessment of the claimant's psychological makeup, but can equally serve to identify the individual presenting. Some experts will take photographs of the person appearing before them and attach it to the report.[4] Most experts now record the formal identification provided by the patient – their driving licence,

---

1   He gave evidence in Cuban heels.

2   One still sees the occasional report which simply gives the claimant's age, although I have never understood why a reporting doctor would not take a date of birth.

3   That said, a report which identifies the claimant by reference to his heavy tattoos and bilateral nipple rings can, of course, give the impression that the reporting doctor has no intention of providing a sympathetic analysis.

4   Although one should bear in mind that the photograph needs to be of decent quality if the report is to be copied repeatedly during the course of the litigation.

passport or other photographic ID is not an unreasonable request to make of a claimant, although there will be those who have no passport and who don't drive, so one also sees utility bills and the like. A copy of the letter from the solicitor asking the patient to attend the appointment is hardly compelling evidence.

DIAGNOSIS

When an individual sees a doctor, he is, perhaps, most interested in the diagnosis in the first instance: "What is wrong with me, doctor?" Of course, in the medico-legal context, the main issue is probably just as likely to be that of prognosis, but it is worth proper consideration of how a doctor might reach a diagnosis which will stand up to scrutiny.

The investigating doctor has to use the various sources of information available before reaching a conclusion on the balance of probabilities. The main sources are threefold:

1. The history given by the claimant;
2. The medical records;
3. Findings on examination.

The history given by the claimant

This is not just his history of the accident, or the presenting complaint, but also the information he provides about his pre-morbid state. A claimant might be able to give a detailed explanation of how his neck hurt after the accident, how he took painkillers, sought out massage and physiotherapy, gradually improved over time and eventually realised that he had recovered. If, of course, he says that he's never had an injury before and it transpires that he has actually made 3 separate claims, 2 in the last 6 months and 1 in respect of an accident a week before, his credibility is likely to be somewhat undermined.

Moreover, if he is describing a high speed accident when the reality is that there was nothing but a trivial scratch to the vehicles, that is going to be fundamental to the formation of the expert's opinion, and if it transpires that the accident was, in fact, minor, the conclusions will potentially fall away.

From the lawyer's point of view, there is no excuse for failing to take a proper history from a claimant. Indeed, the claimant has to approve the report, so there should be two, if not more, opportunities to make sure that the history is right. Unfortunately, claimants rarely seem to read the reports carefully before disclosing them, and the experts themselves are often guilty of sub-optimal history taking. This is a particular problem when there are multiple people in the car and they are seen together and the temptation to cut and paste becomes too much. The same problems arise with claims advanced by minors, where the parent (normally the litigation friend) provides the history to the doctor, irrespective of whether they were present in the car, or in a position to give the requisite evidence. There are similar issues when there is a communication problem between expert and claimant.

However, the real problem is one of sloppy or lazy reporting on the part of the doctor. The nature of low grade medico-legal work is that it is repetitive and rewards the efficient, rather than the painstakingly accurate. The same format is used for all reports. The same standard phrases are used in every report. Often questionnaires are completed before the interview, and whilst there is no difficulty with taking an initial history in that manner, that has to be checked, directly, with the claimant. One often sees reports which say: "This history was recorded in the presence of the claimant and he confirmed that he agreed the same." That is a simple way to ensure that the history given is certified as accurate. If, at a later date, it transpires that it was not, the problem lies with the claimant. Equally, if the report bears that phrase, a solicitor should, as a matter of course, ask the claimant to confirm that that too was true.

What is clear is that if a claimant serves a report where the factual content of the report is wrong, the onus will be on him to explain why the report was served in that form rather than amended. The answer might well be "I told my solicitor that and he wrote to the doctor who declined to change it" but that should be identified at an early stage, preferably before it is served, and certainly by the time of exchange of evidence. One hears the answer all too often in cross-examination, and whilst it might be true, by that time it's too late.

The medical records

These, of course, are not always available. Indeed, as we have seen, there is now a presumption that they will not be obtained in low value claims. The reason, of course, is that defendants felt that the costs outweighed the benefits, although there are cases where they take issue with the claimant's credibility and ask to see the records in any event. Whilst there is an element of having one's cake and eating it, the reality is that only relevant records need to be considered, and the issue of what is relevant is normally fairly clear cut.

The import of the medical records is huge: Did the claimant actually seek treatment when he says he did? What did he tell the doctors about his accident? Did he mention the sites of pain which he latterly claims were injured? Did he attend the doctor with other complaints whilst not mentioning his current problems? Does he, in fact, have a long history of similar, or related complaints which cast doubt on his assertions about causation of his current injuries? Have there been subsequent accidents?

Against that background, it is astonishing that any reporting doctor would want to opine without seeing the notes, but in cases where there is a suggestion of a recent previous accident, particularly if it is one which gives rise to a claim, to report without calling for at least the medical report or notes in respect of that accident is, it must be submitted, negligent. No reasonable treating doctor, faced with the suggestion of a recent previous problem with the injured body part would ignore that information, and no reporting doctor, faced with the suggestion that a previous accident a matter of weeks before which gave rise to equivalent symptoms which miraculously resolved a week before the current accident can safely ignore that information, yet they do so, and do so repeatedly. It fundamentally undermines the credibility of the expert. At the very least, that particular report will be rendered worthless and the claimant will lose out, but with the advent of Qualified One Way Costs Shifting and the possibility of third party costs orders, there will come a time when the aggressive insurer, disgruntled by its inability to recover costs against the claimant, looks to the reporting doctor to see whether their conduct has, in fact, caused the action to proceed when it should not have done so. The technicalities of that sort of application are beyond this volume, but the reporting expert who ignores that sort of clue can only have himself to blame.

Findings on examination

As set out above, one might reasonably expect the recordings of an examination to include the basics of the patient's description. Failing to identify that the claimant was 8 months pregnant when she came in to complain about back pain from a road traffic accident 5 months ago is hardly the basis of a credible opinion, and limiting one's examination to the supposedly injured body part is simply not good enough. In the case of an orthopaedic report or other medical report where a physical examination is required, one might reasonably expect consideration of the shape of the body part, comparison to the other side of the body if appropriate, whether there is any swelling, colour change, temperature change, complaint of pain or discomfort, muscle spasm and a consideration of the range of movement, preferably by reference to normality. Some of those complaints constitute signs – objectively identifiable changes – whilst some will be symptoms – subjective complaints. In the latter case, one might reasonably undertake distraction testing to see whether the complaint is consistent. The old line: "And how far were you able to lift your arm before the accident?" is a straight-forward example of distraction testing, but if a patient cannot rotate his neck by more than 20° on formal testing, but can look over his shoulder to answer a question, there is something wrong. Restricted straight-leg raising by somebody who can sit upright on the couch is another such test. Waddell's signs were habitually recorded by examining doctors 20 years ago, but current reports regularly suggest that the claimant has grossly restricted movement in each and every plane of movement, notwithstanding that such an injury would be both highly improbable and grossly disabling. The suggestion that the patient still has muscle spasm affecting his entire back after 12 months is, again, not compelling, and experts who don't comment on such findings or explain them do not do themselves any favours when it comes to their credibility.

Equally, in non-orthopaedic cases, testing for a consistency of complaint should be an inherent part of assessing a patient's credibility. If the patient denies any previous psychiatric history when, in fact, they were already on antidepressants at the date of the accident, one has to identify that problem and deal with it. There might be reasons why the patient misinformed the doctor, but the doctor should be making clear the need for truth in the answers. Returning to the Pendulum, can the doctor exclude the possibility that the claimant has none of the symptoms of which he complains? If he is not truthful about his history, can he be believed in his report of his symptoms?

CAUSATION

This is often a thorny issue, particularly when there is little or no objective sign of injury. It suits a claimant to say that his injuries were caused by the accident in question, because that permits him to claim compensation, but can the expert confirm that? The first point is that the test is on the balance of probabilities, but even then the burden is on the claimant to persuade the court that he was injured as he says.

At this point, one needs to return to the analysis of the Pendulum. Can one exclude the possibility that the claimant has all the symptoms of which he complains, but none of them was caused by the accident? Scans and x-rays are not determinative, because musculoskeletal deterioration is commonplace and does not necessarily correlate with reported symptoms. Equally, if there are underlying changes, would they have become symptomatic in due course in any event? Is there a constitutional weakness? Is that a case of taking the claimant as you find them, or has the accident simply brought forward those symptoms? Are the symptoms now worse than they would have been had they come about naturally? What would have caused the claimant to become symptomatic had this accident not occurred, and when? All of these questions should be considered in reaching a conclusion about the diagnosis (acknowledging that the answers also potentially stray into the question of prognosis).

The position can get even more complicated in, for instance, cases of psychiatric injury, where the diagnosis is dependent upon which of the necessary criteria have been fulfilled. There is potentially a range of opinion as to whether a particular complaint satisfies the requirements for that specific diagnosis, and the fact that what is most important to a claimant on any given day might change can lead to differences of opinion from the experts as to the label to be put on the condition, even if the overall effects on the claimant and the treatment required might be very similar.

The key for the expert, whatever his field of specialism, is to explain both why he has reached the diagnosis and what the diagnosis actually means in the real world. He has to draw the balance between accuracy and simplicity. Saying that the patient suffered pain as a result of the accident is not a diagnosis, it is a repetition of his history. If the claimant is reporting a lower back injury from a rear end shunt, is it really appropriate to diagnose a whiplash injury? It gives the impression that the expert is not giving proper consideration to his reporting.

PROGNOSIS

A high proportion of personal injury litigation falls to be determined under the Pre-Action Protocol for Low Value Personal Injury Claims in Road Traffic Accidents from 31 July 2013 (see chapter 5), via the MOJ Portal and, if necessary, a Stage 3 hearing where the appropriate valuation is determined by the court.

In those circumstances, much turns on the prognosis proffered by the examining doctor. If the opinion is that the claimant should recover in 9 months, and the claimant says that it was nearer 12, the court is unlikely to go beyond the expert's opinion. If, of course, the claimant is honest and admits to recovering in 6 months, the court will assess damages on that less generous basis.

Logically, if the expert's opinion represents an average recovery period, roughly half of their patients will recover earlier than expected, whilst the rest will not recover in the suggested time period. Potentially 50% of patients should be returning to the medical expert complaining that they have not recovered within the requisite time period.

That, of course, creates a problem for the reporting doctor, particularly where the entire system is now aimed at assessing damages based on one, fixed price, report. The temptation, particularly if one is preparing large numbers of reports, often for the same solicitors, is to give the claimant the benefit of the doubt and tend towards generosity in terms of the prognosis period. After all, if one underestimates the recovery period, more work will be required and there are risks that the second report will be deemed inappropriate and costs not recovered. The question will then be asked by the solicitors as to why the doctor thought that the claimant would recover more swiftly than was, in fact, the case.

If, on the other hand, the claimant recovers more quickly, the expert is overstating the injury with the effect of potentially increasing the value of the claim (and the costs recovered by those who instruct him). It would be naïve to believe that claimants will voluntarily accept less money than is being offered, or that their lawyers will go out of their way to ensure that their clients get less. It is all too easy to get the client to sign a standard form witness statement confirming that he agrees the contents of the report, safe in the knowledge that he will not be cross-examined, particularly when the costs available to the lawyers are so limited.

It is this precise conundrum which has caused the recent public debates about soft tissue injuries in road traffic accidents, but that level of political commentary is beyond the scope of this book.

What can be said is this: If 99% of patients recover within the proposed timescale, the reports are too generous. That sort of accuracy (backed up with an amazingly high number of claimants who concur that the expert was absolutely right in his estimate as to when they would recover) suggests that the expert is not, in fact, reporting properly.

The provision of a prognosis is not the only 'range of opinion' which should be addressed by an expert, as we have already seen. Many report writers seem to think that by saying that a whiplash injury, assessed within 6 weeks of the accident, will take 12 – 18 months to resolve, they have provided a range of opinion and have fulfilled their duties to the court. They have not, as we have seen, set out the full range of opinion, but until the courts themselves take issue with the quality of reporting, the problem will continue.

What is actually meant by the prognosis figure? A good proportion of the population suffer daily aches and pains which are nothing to do with whether they have been involved in an accident, but simply pertain to the human condition. At what point does a person's cause for complaint cease to be (objectively) related to the accident? Logically, if there are potential idiopathic aches, how can one opine that the claimant will ever be symptom-free? The answer lies in the balance of probabilities.

The reporting expert should, in assessing a soft tissue injury, not only consider the veracity of the presentation, but also the fact that a person who is seeking compensation has motive to maximise his symptoms. He should address whether he perceives a difference between those patients seen for medico-legal reports and those seeking treatment. He should consider whether the claimant has not, in fact, been injured, either to the extent claimed, or at all. If he does not address those matters, he has not set out the range of opinion. If he has not excluded those matters, his report arguably falls short of the requirements of 35PD.

Whilst there are arguments to counter that, the reality is that they are based on cost, cost-efficiency, the integrity of the system and the fact that if an expert starts challenging the veracity of clients, they will lose the work. That is the nub of the problem. Unfortunately, the failure to address that problem might yet see the end of that sort of medico-legal work. By raising the quality of the reports provided, experts can safeguard themselves against criticism. That, in turn, leads to an enhanced reputation which can only lead to more work.

Format and Contents

The basic structure of such a report is fairly standardised, albeit that a significant proportion of reports fail in one or more regards.

1. The writer identifies the subject of the report and should provide appropriate data, to include the client's name, address and date of birth, the date of the accident, the date of the examination, the place of the examination, the date of the report (if different). One habitually sees reports which do not contain the date of the accident, or simply give the current age of the claimant, although this last is less common than it used to be. He should also identify who has instructed him and, although this is relatively rarely seen, the medical agency through which he has received instructions if that is the case. There is no formal requirement for these pieces of information, but they represent good practice and are transparent. More importantly, they identify the report as being accurate and as having been written anew, whereas where the dates are wrong, or the male claimant is referred to as 'she' the suspicion is that this is a *pro forma* report where little, if any, consideration has actually gone into it. The problem that arises is that the client then has to either go to the trouble of correcting the expert's English, or accepts a report which is patently wrong.

2. The writer's qualifications need to be set out, either at the start of the report or by way of an Appendix. As set out in Chapter 2, those qualifications should justify his role as a medico-legal expert in the context of the instant report.

3. The report should identify its purpose, which, as referenced elsewhere, is a simple, but underused, technique to ensure that the questions being asked are the right ones in all the circumstances. That purpose should, in reality, be extended to include an assessment, insofar as is possible, of the consistency and credibility of the claimant's account.

4. The expert should confirm the means by which he communicated with the client, and whether there was anybody else in the room. One often sees children examined in the presence of their parents, but there is no attempt to obtain a history from the child, even though they might be 14 years old. The impression is that the parent simply gives a version of events which are accepted as true, without any means of telling whether they are accurate.

5. The client's history should then be set out clearly and, preferably, in the words of the client. Often that history is dictated in the presence of the client, who confirms its accuracy. The modern trend seems to be more of a drop down menu, which gives the impression that the reports are wholly artificial. Every claimant is said to be a regular gym attender who was unable to go after the accident. Either going to the gym increases the risk of one being involved in, and injured in, an accident, or there is a standard question to which people answer yes to try to support the contention that they were injured, when in fact, that isn't true. The problem going forwards is that with section 57 of the Criminal Justice and Courts Act 2015 potentially depriving a legitimate claimant of the entirety of his damages if he is found, on balance, to be fundamentally dishonest in one respect of this claim, an inaccurate report, unchallenged by the solicitors (perhaps because of cost-efficiency) and unchallenged by the claimant (perhaps because of laziness) can prove to be a significant problem, caused and maintained by the manner in which the expert takes the history.

   One issue which has arisen is the expert who tells the client what his injuries were. One client with a nasty rotator cuff (shoulder) injury was informed by the expert that he'd probably injured his lower back. The client left the examination, only for the expert to produce a report about a low back injury and ask for payment! Dictating the history in the presence of the claimant avoids any possible misunderstanding, as long as the parties are able to communicate.

6. The client's previous medical history needs to be taken in full. This is a huge potential pitfall for the unwary, because the claimant whose

report declares no previous accidents when, in fact, he had one 2 weeks before the instant accident, or, worse still, between the accident which is the subject of the examination and the examination itself, leaves the claimant's credibility in tatters. The questions that need to be asked, and more importantly recorded as having been asked, should be specific – Have you had any other accidents or claims in the last *x* years? Have you previously suffered from any neck or back pain? Have you seen your doctor with neck or back pain in the last *x* years? Have you had any accidents since this one? Did you have any symptoms in the week or so before this accident? Were you taking any medication? Can you think of any other potential cause of your pain? These are not difficult questions, and they would be asked by a competent treating doctor, so why not in the case of a medico-legal report?

7. The findings on examination need to be recorded. The expert should comment on the consistency of those findings. If the claimant presents with 20° of straight leg raise, but can sit comfortably on the couch, why not say so? If the client appears to be unable to move his neck in any direction, but managed to drive to the examination, say so. There seems to be a fear amongst doctors that if they give an honest assessment of the clients, they will lose work, and their solicitors will lose money, but if there is a credibility issue, that needs to be explored at the earliest possible stage, before significant legal costs are incurred. Moreover, in some cases the reason for the inconsistent presentation is one of aetiology – if there is a functional overlay that needs to be identified and addressed, not brushed under the carpet as an inconvenience.

8. The relevant entries in the medical records, if available, should be set out on the face of the report. They should include the fact of unrelated attendances on the GP at or about the time of the accident. If a claimant visits his GP 4 times before he complains of disabling neck pain, that should be recorded, because it is clearly pertinent to the claimant's credibility. In the case of more serious injuries, x-rays, scans, theatre notes and the like will need to be considered and set out in detail. If there is a risk of long-term degeneration, the expert

will need to see updated scans in due course to judge the progress of the injury over time.

9. The expert should then opine as to whether or not the client was injured, the nature of that injury, the cause of that injury and the likely prognosis for that injury. In answering those questions, he would do well to start with the Pendulum analysis and reject the non-answers, with reasons. In assessing the likely prognosis for the injury, he should identify the factors which tend to influence recovery and identify how he has reached his view. If he is going to recommend physiotherapy (so often not taken up that one wonders whether there was any need) he needs to identify the effect on the recovery period and the reasons why it would be beneficial.

The Range of Opinion

The detailed analysis of the concept of the Range of Opinion set out in Chapter 10 stems, in the most part, from medico-legal reporting of this ilk and there is little to be gained from repeating it here. Similarly, this chapter has already considered some of the issues which arise. There are two specific points which are worth considering in slightly more detail.

The first scenario is where the claimant has an underlying condition, which may or may not have been symptomatic before the accident, but which has been worsened by the accident, either by having been brought forward or by having been accelerated. From a medico-legal perspective, such cases are often referred to as 'acceleration' cases although often the experts acknowledge that the condition itself has not been accelerated, just the onset of symptoms from that condition. That, in itself, is a nuanced distinction. The answer lies in the Pendulum. Some of the symptoms are caused by the accident, some are not. The extent to which the symptoms are accident-related can be identified by any credible pre-accident history of symptoms (or lack thereof), the findings on objective examination and the likely progression of such signs absent an injury. It is, ultimately, an opinion, expressed by somebody who has observed similar patients for many years. If one excludes possibilities, it is possible to narrow down the range of opinion before alighting on a specific answer, and it is always worth bearing in mind that the court has to decide on the balance of probabilities, rather than absolutes. The more detailed the reasons for alighting on an answer, even if the starting point is to reject the alternatives, the more compelling an answer will be.

The second situation is where an injury might deteriorate over time. There, the main difficulties are in assessing the timescale over which that deterioration might occur, the speed and extent of that deterioration and the likely effect in terms of the need for surgery and the like. Very often those questions get elided so that there is an answer that there is "a 40% chance of osteoarthritis in the next 15 years", but there is no answer to what the chance is over 5 years, or over 25 years, or whether that will progress to a point where surgery is required. The lawyers potentially want to know when, on balance, the claimant will have to give up work; when, on balance, he will need surgery and the cost of that; whether there will be a need for revision surgery and the likely cost and timing of that. That evidence is required to value the claim but often the reporting doctor is concentrating on the medical aspects of the case without an appreciation of the legal aspects. The onus, in the first instance, should be on the instructing party (or his lawyers) to identify the specific questions to be asked, but the expert should be aware of the use to which his report is to be put. If there is any doubt as to the questions to be asked and answered, that should be addressed before the report is finalised.

One method for setting out the risks of degeneration over time might be to ask the following questions:

a. Is this an injury which almost inevitably leads to deterioration?
b. Is this an injury which is more likely than not to lead to a deterioration? What are the chances of that coming to pass?
c. Is this an injury which could deteriorate, but is more likely not to? If so, what are the chances of deterioration?

    d. If this injury is going to deteriorate, over what period of time is it likely to deteriorate? At what point in time is it more likely than not to become symptomatic?

    e. At what point in time would the expert opine that if the injury remains asymptomatic it is likely to remain that way;

    f. If the injury is going to deteriorate, what are the chances that it will require medical intervention? In respect of any specific type of treatment, what are the chances that would be required and when would it be more likely than to be required? What are the costs and likely effects of that treatment? Would there be a need for further treatment?

Other areas of medical expertise will have particular questions which regularly arise. If this particular individual has a pre-existing vulnerability, what might one have expected to happen in any event, when, and why? Conducting that analysis against the background of the Pendulum offers the expert a solid foundation from which to opine.

CHAPTER TWENTY
MEDICAL REPORTS
(ENT (NIHL))

Whilst there are a host of circumstances in which the evidence of an ENT surgeon (or Otolaryngologist) might be required, in recent years claims for Noise Induced Hearing Loss (whether deafness and/or tinnitus) have come to the fore. There is a sizeable cohort of (predominantly blue-collar) workers who were employed in noisy environments, without hearing protection, often working long hours with power tools or against background noise, who now complain of deafness. Human frailty being what it is, there is an inevitable deterioration of hearing with age (presbyacusis, or A(ge) A(ssociated) H(earing) (L)oss)) such that in many cases, whilst the hearing loss was suffered some time ago, it is only in later life that the noise-induced hearing loss (NIHL), compounded with the ongoing AAHL, reaches a level which causes noticeable problems.

Against that, of course, is the question of Limitation. If somebody has particularly poor hearing, the likelihood is that they will have realised that some considerable time ago, and their likely date of knowledge for the purposes of section 14 of the Limitation Act 1980 is sufficiently historic that the claim is time-barred. That is not to say that they will be aware of the extent of their problems. If they work in a noisy environment and always have, and live alone, they might never get to grips with their hearing loss, because it is not something one discusses with strangers.

From a legal perspective, exposure to excessive noise before the publication of *Noise and the Worker* (1963) is unlikely to be 'negligent' exposure, but from 1963 onwards employers were deemed aware of the risks to their employees' hearing from excessive noise. The Noise at Work Regulations 1989 (which came into force on 1 January 1990) provided a more stringent framework for employers which has since been tightened yet further by The Control of Noise at Work Regulations 2005, requiring protection for employees at progressively lower thresholds.

The question of whether a defendant has breached its duty to an employee is often the subject of engineering evidence, which is dealt with elsewhere, but, inherent in any such claim are a number of medical issues which fall to be dealt with by the medical expert and in respect of which there is plenty of scope for disagreement.

In 2000, Coles, Lutman and Buffin published a paper, *'Guidelines on the diagnosis of noise-induced hearing loss for medicolegal purposes'* ('CLB') which attempted to analyse whether, in any given case, it was more likely than not that an individual had suffered NIHL. There is some debate about whether those guidelines are too generous to claimants, or should not be applied in certain cases, and in 2015, Lutman, Coles and Buffin published a second paper *'Guidelines for quantification of noise-induced hearing loss in a medicolegal context'* which finesses the analysis of the quantification of noise induced hearing loss, rather than the diagnosis of noise induced hearing loss (the clues being in the titles of the respective papers).[1]

The starting point in any such analysis is the taking of an audiogram under proper test conditions and then analysing both the shape and the absolute nature of that audiogram. For those unfamiliar with audiometric testing, the subject is positioned in a quiet room, wearing suitable headphones, through which a pure tone of given frequency is played, and is asked to indicate, by pressing a button, when he is aware of the sound. The volume is increased, normally by 10dB at a time, to a point when the subject can hear the sound, and then dropped (normally by 5dB at a time) and, if necessary, raised again, to try to ensure that the test result is consistent. This is repeated for both ears at a number of different frequencies, depending on the circumstances of the test. The results can then be plotted on a graph (although sometimes the results are simply tabulated). If in graph form, the x axis has the various frequencies, whilst the y axis shows the volume in decibels (dB). The y axis

---

1   There are, of course, numerous other papers, but they are the remit of the experts themselves and are beyond this book.

is inverted so that the higher numbers are at the bottom, so that if a subject requires a particular frequency to be at a higher volume before he can hear it (because he is deaf at that particular level), the line on the graph drops at that point, signifying that his hearing is worse.

The relevant questions

The nuances of such testing is beyond the scope of this work, but the relevant questions in such cases tend, ultimately, to boil down to these:

1. What, objectively tested, is the state of the claimant's hearing? What are the circumstances of the audiometry?

2. Does that constitute a hearing loss above and beyond that which might be expected for someone of the claimant's age and gender? Against what data set should the comparison be made and why?

3. Does the pattern of that hearing loss suggest that it has, on balance, been caused or contributed to by exposure to excessive noise?

4. Is there any need and/or benefit and/or additional information gleaned from additional testing, to include bone-conduction tests or otherwise? If not, why not?

5. Does the expert opine on the basis of CLB or on some other basis? If he rejects the CLB, why?

6. What is the materiality and/or effect of a loss at 4kHz?

7. What is the materiality and/or effect of losses at other frequencies?

8. Is there any other exposure to noise other than at work?

9. If there is an element of NIHL present, what part of the claimant's hearing loss is caused by exposure to excessive noise? Is there any other apparent cause?

10. Is there a change in the claimant's presentation over time? If so, what is the cause of that? Should one be averaging the audiometry results?

11. Is there an objective asymmetry in the presentation? If so, what is the cause of that?

12. What is the nature and extent of the tinnitus (if any)? What is the cause of the tinnitus?

13. Is there a need for aiding? If so, to what extent has that requirement been brought forward? How would aiding benefit the claimant?

That is not to say that there are not other points to be taken, but from the medical point of view, whether one is looking at the question of causation or the extent of the hearing loss, those questions offer a starting point to the analysis. It is, of course, a slightly more refined analysis of the Pendulum, but the core issues remain.

Format and Contents

Of course, before one gets to that analysis, a reporting doctor should have a history from the claimant, which covers *inter alia* his family history,[2] his exposure to noise other than at work, his working practices (to include the types of machines used, the hours worked and the provision of hearing protection), when and in what circumstances he noticed the onset of his problems, and the effect and progression of those symptoms. Face to face testing might give an impression of whether an individual has specific problems, and a picture is thereby built up, which is either consistent with, or inconsistent with, a diagnosis of NIHL.

---

2 A family history of deafness can raise various issues. It might be that the parents worked in the same factory as the claimant. They might have had illness or genetically poor hearing. Their own deafness might have rendered it more difficult for the claimant to identify his own problems, because, if he were still living at home, his opportunity for quiet conversation outside the workplace would not have occurred.

Having taken that history, and reviewed the audiogram (one would normally take an audiogram as part of the examination), together with any historical audiometry (if the defendant has managed to get around to providing same), the expert can then start to address the questions outlined above. In each case, there is no reason why one should not set out the range of opinions before identifying the preferred conclusion. If there is a requirement for more data, he can identify such other tests as he might need. Indeed, one might argue that he is under a duty so to do.

One should never forget that whilst the lawyer commissioning such a report is, on balance, somebody with an above average knowledge and understanding of the issues in such a case, if the case is to proceed to trial, it might be heard by somebody who has no understanding of the issues in the case. To that end, and bearing in mind that, certainly from a claimant's perspective, such reports are in a relatively standardised form, I see no reason not to include a basic explanation of how and why damage at certain frequencies might affect a person's hearing.

That should include a basic explanation of the baseline frequencies of certain types of noise might be. The 250Hz reading on the audiogram approximates to Middle C on the piano, with each octave halving or doubling the frequency. A man singing Bass might be using a range between 80Hz and, perhaps, 350Hz whilst a Soprano's range takes one to 1kHz or so ("Top C" is approximately 1046Hz).

There is, however, a difference between being able to tell whether some-body is speaking and deciphering what is actually being said. Certain sounds are, superficially, similar, and the differentiation between those similar sounds actually occurs at a higher frequency, normally north of 1kHz, so the listener's ability to determine the sound within the noise is important. If the hearing is damaged at the 1kHz level, it compromises the ability to detect the difference in sounds, so that the speaker's voice sounds mumbled. The listener then compromises, by (in the case of listening to the radio or television) by turning up the sound. In the case of a conversation, one looks at the lips of the speaker to try to determ-ine the sounds being made.

To include a relatively basic explanation of hearing is, superficially, below the pay grade for an ENT Consultant, but it is important to understand that the reader of a report may need that assistance, if only to have the background against which to judge the issues in the case. Similarly, an explanation of the decibel scale and what it actually means, both in objective terms and subjective terms, will inevitably engage the tribunal which can only serve to increase the interest in the critical contents of the report.

Range of Opinion

One of the main difficulties with determining whether a claimant has NIHL is that there are other causes for hearing loss beyond exposure to noise and the effects of age. Certain medical conditions or medications can cause damage to one's hearing, and, because one is trying to determine cause from effect, rather than direct, visual inspection, a diagnosis of idiopathic loss is far more common than in other types of personal injury claim. From a defendant's perspective, the prospect that a claimant's loss can legitimately be described as idiopathic (arising spontaneously or for which the cause is unknown) means that a claimant cannot simply say: "I was exposed to noise and my hearing is worse than one might have thought, so it must be noise related." That, in turn, means that a defendant has, more than might normally arise, a vested interest in simply undermining the claimant's case, rather than putting up an alternative theory.

It becomes ever more important, particularly from a claimant's perspective, that a rigid analysis, based on the range of opinion, is undertaken, not least because if one accepts that there might be contrary views, but can show why one rejects them, particularly if concessions are made as appropriate, the alternative view which might seek to dismiss each and every point in the claimant's favour makes the attacker look unreasonable. The alternative, which is to pretend that the counter-arguments do not exist, can only lay one open to criticism.

With that in mind, it is worth considering the questions posited above. They are not exhaustive, but they do not preclude a conclusion one way or another – they merely offer signage by which the analysis might be mapped.

CONCLUSION

No book on experts could hope to cover every field of expertise. Within the personal injury field, there are any number of medical specialities, and experts who assist with the valuation of claims, such as Care experts, Occupational Therapists, Orthotics, Accountants, Architects and Employment Consultants. Beyond the personal injury field, we have Valuers, Foreign Law experts, Security & Risk Analysis consultants, DNA experts and Statisticians. The list is very long indeed, but the problems which arise, and the principles which should be applied, are the same.

The Civil Procedure Rules, now nearly 20 years old, were meant to change the way in which expert evidence was obtained and received. Whilst there was, initially, a change in mindset from many experts who saw the need to change their ways as the only to survive, it is, once again, all too common to see reports which adopt a partisan point of view, paying only lip service to the duty to the court. It is to be hoped that by highlighting those failings and offering guidance as to the production of reports that the quality of expert evidence will improve and that the basic premise of CPR35 will, eventually, be fulfilled. Whether that will happen or not, is a matter of opinion.

MORE BOOKS BY
LAW BRIEF PUBLISHING

'A Practical Guide to Holiday Sickness Claims' by Andrew Mckie & Ian Skeate
'Ellis and Kevan on Credit Hire, 5th Edition' by Aidan Ellis & Tim Kevan
'RTA Allegations of Fraud in a Post-Jackson Era: The Handbook, 2nd Edition' by Andrew Mckie
'RTA Personal Injury Claims: A Practical Guide Post-Jackson' by Andrew Mckie
'A Practical Guide to Personal Injuries in Sport' by Adam Walker & Patricia Leonard
'A Practical Approach to Clinical Negligence Post-Jackson' by Geoffrey Simpson-Scott
'A Practical Guide to Costs in Personal Injury Cases' by Matthew Hoe
'Occupiers, Highways and Defective Premises Claims: A Practical Guide Post-Jackson' by Andrew Mckie
'Employers' Liability Claims: A Practical Guide Post-Jackson' by Andrew Mckie
'A Practical Guide to Subtle Brain Injury Claims' by Pankaj Madan
'Baby Steps: A Guide to Maternity Leave and Maternity Pay' by Leah Waller
'The Queen's Counsel Lawyer's Omnibus: 20 Years of Cartoons from the Times 1993-2013' by Alex Steuart Williams

These books and more are available to order online direct from the publisher at www.lawbriefpublishing.com, where you can also read free sample chapters. For any queries, contact us on 0844 587 2383 or mail@lawbriefpublishing.com.

Our books are also usually in stock at www.amazon.co.uk with free next day delivery for Prime members, and at good legal bookshops such as Hammicks and Wildy & Sons.

We are regularly launching new books in our series of practical day-to-day practitioners' guides. Visit our website and join our free newsletter to be kept informed.

Printed in Great Britain
by Amazon